IDIOMS
ORIGINS & MEANINGS

A Dictionary of Popular Sayings, Phrases and Expressions

By Jasper Hartwell

1st Edition

Ferros Publishing © 2023

Author: Jasper Hartwell

ISBN: 9798864660942

Disclaimer

Introduction

Idioms, those quirky combinations of words that convey so much more than their individual parts might suggest, are the seasoning of language. They color conversations, add depth to narratives, and provide a window into the soul of a culture. Across different languages and societies, idioms reflect shared human experiences, while also highlighting unique local customs, tales, and beliefs.

This book takes you on a voyage across time and continents, exploring the origins and evolutions of some of the most colorful idioms. From the trials and tribulations of historic battles to daily life in ancient marketplaces, from poetic inspirations to myths handed down through generations, every idiom has a story to tell.

Prepare to be intrigued by linguistic mysteries, entertained by surprising tales, and enlightened about the contexts in which these idioms were born. By the end of this journey, not only will you have enriched your linguistic arsenal, but you'll also gain a deeper appreciation for the incredible tapestry of culture, history, and human creativity that language can hold.

So, whether you're a word enthusiast, a curious soul, or someone looking to spice up their conversations, this book is your passport to a world where words dance, histories come alive, and every phrase is a story waiting to be told. Dive in and let the journey begin!

Table of Contents

Nature and Animals

When Pigs Fly

The phrase "when pigs fly" is used to describe an event or action that is deemed impossible or highly unlikely to ever happen.

Origin

The idiom's origin is rooted in the age-old idea that certain things are inherently impossible, with the flight of pigs being one such example due to their anatomy and weight. The concept of pigs flying has long been used in various cultures as a humorous representation of impossibility.

There are several theories and historical references to the idiom:

1. Old Proverbs and Sayings: The idea of pigs flying has been used for centuries. The idiom can be traced back to old Scottish and English proverbs that imply impossibility or incredulity. An example from the late 1500s is "pigs fly in the air with their tails forward."

2. Literary References: The concept appears in literature, such as Lewis Carroll's "Alice's Adventures in Wonderland" (1865). The Duchess tells Alice, "Thinking again?" the Duchess asked, with another dig of her sharp little chin. "I've a right to think," said Alice sharply... "Just about as much right," said the Duchess, "as pigs have to fly."

3. Cultural Variations: Many cultures have their own version of this idiom. For instance, in Germany, they say, "when pigs whistle" and in Russia, it's "when the crayfish whistles on the mountain."

Example Sentence

"You think he'll start exercising and eating healthy? Yeah, maybe when pigs fly!"

The enduring popularity of this idiom underscores its effectiveness in humorously conveying skepticism or disbelief. It's a playful way of saying, "That's never going to happen."

Wild Goose Chase

Meaning

The term "wild goose chase" refers to a futile or fruitless pursuit or search, an endeavor that is likely to be without results or a task that is seen as pointless.

Origin

The origins of the phrase "wild goose chase" might be a bit surprising to some, as its initial meaning was quite different from the current usage:

1. Horse Racing and Shakespeare: The original reference to a "wild goose chase" comes from the 16th century and was a type of horse race. In this race, riders followed a lead horse, mimicking the way wild geese follow their leader in flight. It wasn't about catching something but rather following in a particular path, much like geese in migration. The term was popularized by William Shakespeare in his play "Romeo and Juliet" (Act 2, Scene 4).

2. Evolution of Meaning: Over time, the meaning of the phrase shifted. Instead of referring to a specific kind of race, it began to take on the connotation of a fruitless or pointless pursuit, perhaps because of the inherent unpredictability and difficulty in tracking wild geese.

Example Sentence

"Searching for the original manuscript in the vast library turned out to be a wild goose chase."

Today, when someone refers to a "wild goose chase," they're often speaking about an effort that's expected to be lengthy, challenging, and potentially without a satisfactory outcome.

Walking on Thin Ice

Meaning

The idiom "walking on thin ice" is used to describe someone who is in a precarious or risky situation, or someone who is taking risks that might result in trouble or danger.

Origin

The phrase originates from the literal danger associated with walking on ice that's too thin to support a person's weight. If the ice is too thin, it could crack and the individual could fall into the cold water beneath, facing life-threatening conditions.

1. Literal Context: In colder regions, lakes, rivers, and ponds freeze over during winter. While the ice can often support the weight of a person, it's not always consistently thick across the entire surface. There are areas where the ice might be thinner due to currents, springs, or other factors. Venturing onto these spots is dangerous, and people native to these regions are often taught from a young age to be cautious and recognize the signs of thin ice.

2. Figurative Usage: The danger of walking on literal thin ice, where one wrong step can lead to calamity, made it a fitting metaphor for other risky situations. Over time, this concept was generalized to any scenario where one is treading dangerously or acting in ways that could lead to negative consequences.

Example Sentence

"If you keep skipping team meetings, you're walking on thin ice; the manager might consider it insubordination."

Today, the idiom is widely recognized and used to caution someone against risky behavior or to point out that they're in a potentially perilous situation. It's a vivid metaphor that effectively communicates the idea of risk and the need for caution.

The Early Bird Catches the Worm

Meaning

The idiom "The early bird catches the worm" conveys the idea that those who take prompt action or arrive first are most likely to succeed or gain an advantage. Essentially, it emphasizes the benefits of being proactive and taking initiative.

Origin

This saying's origin is deeply rooted in agrarian societies and the observation of nature:

1. Nature and Agriculture: The phrase takes inspiration from the natural world, where birds that start their search for food early in the day have a better chance of finding worms than those that start late. Worms tend to come out at dawn, so birds that are up and active at this time can easily find and consume them.

2. Historical Usage: The proverb has been in use in English since at least the 17th century. One of its earliest recorded uses is from a 1670 collection of proverbs by John Ray, where it's listed as "The early bird catcheth the worm." Over time, this has evolved into the more familiar "catches" rather than "catcheth."

3. Cultural Resonance: Beyond its agrarian origins, the idiom also reflects the values of many cultures that prioritize hard work, diligence, and initiative. For societies based on farming, rising early was a necessity to make the most of the daylight hours, especially during planting and harvest seasons.

Example Sentence

"If you want to get those concert tickets, remember: the early bird catches the worm. So, be sure to be online right when they go on sale!"

The phrase is frequently used to motivate and inspire, emphasizing the advantages of being an early riser or getting a head start in endeavors. In the modern context, it's applicable not just to waking up early, but to any situation where acting quickly or being the first to take action can offer benefits.

Let Sleeping Dogs Lie

Meaning

The idiom "let sleeping dogs lie" advises against bringing up old conflicts or problems, or disturbing a situation that is currently stable even if it's not resolved to everyone's satisfaction. The underlying message is that stirring up old issues might result in more harm than good.

Origin

The origins of this idiom can be traced back through centuries and various cultures:

1. Literal Interpretation: At the most basic level, the saying derives from the observation that it's unwise to disturb dogs while they're sleeping because they might react aggressively if suddenly awoken. This simple observation then became a metaphor for potential risks in other situations.

2. Historical Usage: The expression, in various forms, has been in use since the 14th century. One of the earliest written records of this idiom is found in Geoffrey Chaucer's poem "Troilus and Criseyde," which dates back to 1380. The specific line reads, "It is nought good a slepyng hound to wake."

3. Sir Walter Scott's Influence: The modern English version of the phrase can be attributed to the early 19th century. Sir Walter Scott, in his work "Redgauntlet" (published in 1824), wrote: "Better let the wound bleed on—it will be time to look for the scar when it is healed—better let the sleeping dog lie."

Example Sentence

"After so many years, she wanted to discuss why their friendship had ended, but I thought it was best to let sleeping dogs lie."

The idiom embodies a piece of wisdom that transcends cultures: Sometimes, revisiting past grievances or issues, especially when nothing can be changed or remedied, can cause more pain, resentment, or conflict. It's a counsel for discretion and for choosing peace over confrontation in certain circumstances.

A Fish Out of Water

The idiom "a fish out of water" describes someone who is out of their usual place or comfort zone and feels awkward or out of place in a particular situation or environment. It conveys a sense of discomfort, unfamiliarity, or inadaptability.

Origin

The imagery behind this phrase is simple but powerful:

1. Literal Interpretation: Fish live and breathe in water. When taken out of their aquatic environment, they struggle to breathe, become immobile, and generally cannot survive for long. Their distress is evident and immediate. This stark contrast between the fish's natural habitat and its inability to function outside of it forms the basis for the idiom.

2. Historical Usage: While the exact origin of the phrase is hard to pinpoint, the concept has been understood and expressed in literature for centuries. The idea of a fish being out of its natural habitat and struggling is intuitive, making it a universally relatable metaphor.

Example Sentence

"When I moved from the countryside to the big city for college, I felt like a fish out of water. Everything was so unfamiliar and overwhelming."

This idiom resonates because everyone, at some point in their lives, has likely felt out of place or out of their depth. Whether it's starting a new job, moving to a new country, or even joining a new social group, the feeling of being "a fish out of water" is a common human experience. The phrase captures that vulnerability and the challenges of adapting to new environments or situations.

Kill Two Birds with One Stone

Meaning

The idiom "kill two birds with one stone" refers to achieving two objectives or solving two problems with a single action or effort. It emphasizes efficiency and the clever use of resources to obtain multiple benefits.

Origin

The origins of this idiom are somewhat ambiguous, but it can be traced through various cultures and histories:

1. Ancient Origins: Some suggest that the concept behind the idiom has ancient roots. One of the earliest versions can be found in Chinese culture. The Chinese equivalent, 一石二鸟 (yī shí èr niǎo), translates directly to "one stone, two birds" and has been used in Chinese literature for centuries.

2. European Influence: The phrase as we know it might have evolved in Europe. While the exact time of its first use in English is not definitively known, its essence has been present in European cultures for a long time. It's worth noting that similar expressions exist in other European languages too, suggesting a shared cultural appreciation for the idea behind the phrase.

3. Modern Usage: The exact phrasing "kill two birds with one stone" started to appear in English literature in the 1600s. Over time, its use became more widespread, and it was incorporated into everyday language to represent efficiency and multi-tasking.

Example Sentence

"By picking up the dry cleaning on my way to the grocery store, I can kill two birds with one stone and save time on errands."

While the idiom's imagery might seem violent to some modern listeners, especially those sensitive to animal welfare, it's essential to understand it in its historical and cultural context. The phrase has been used metaphorically for centuries to express the idea of efficiency, and its primary focus is on the achievement of multiple objectives, not on the act of harming birds.

Don't Count Your Chickens Before They Hatch

The idiom "don't count your chickens before they hatch" warns against assuming that future events will turn out favorably and acting on such assumptions, especially when those outcomes are not guaranteed. Essentially, it's a caution against being overly optimistic or making premature decisions based on anticipated results.

Origin

The sentiment behind this saying has been around for millennia, and its roots can be traced through different cultures:

1. Aesop's Fables: One of the earliest sources of this phrase is attributed to Aesop's Fables in the tale of "The Milkmaid and Her Pail." In this story, a milkmaid daydreams about the things she'll buy after selling her milk. As she gets lost in her imaginings, she accidentally spills the milk and loses the opportunity to sell it. The moral of the story aligns with the essence of the idiom.

2. Historical Usage: The exact phrasing "don't count your chickens before they're hatched" can be traced back to the 16th century. Thomas Howell, in his work "New Sonnets and Pretty Pamphlets" from 1570, uses a version of this saying, implying that it was a well-understood concept even then.

3. The Farming Connection: The phrase itself draws a vivid picture from the world of farming. Not all eggs laid by a chicken will necessarily hatch into chicks. Various factors can affect an egg's viability, like its age, temperature fluctuations, or potential damage. By assuming every egg will become a chicken, one might miscalculate and be left with fewer chickens than expected.

Example Sentence

"He was so sure his startup would get venture funding, he leased an expensive office space in advance. It's a classic case of counting your chickens before they hatch, as the funding fell through."

The idiom is a timeless reminder to be cautious and not to take future outcomes for granted. It emphasizes the importance of waiting for results before making decisions or celebrating successes.

A Drop in the Ocean

The idiom "a drop in the ocean" (or sometimes "a drop in the bucket") refers to something very small or insignificant, especially when compared to something much larger or more comprehensive. It's often used to describe an effort or contribution that, while possibly valuable in its own right, has minimal impact on the larger situation or problem.

Origin

The imagery and concept behind this idiom draw from a natural and easily understood comparison:

1. Literal Interpretation: If you picture a single drop of water and then compare it to the vastness of the ocean, the drop seems inconsequential. This vivid contrast between the minuteness of the drop and the enormity of the ocean illustrates the heart of the idiom.

2. Biblical Connections: The alternative phrase "a drop in the bucket" appears in the Bible, specifically in the Book of Isaiah (Isaiah 40:15): "Behold, the nations are as a drop of a bucket, and are counted as the small dust of the balance."

3. Historical Usage: Over time, both variations of the idiom have been adopted and adapted in different cultures and languages, underscoring its universality. The phrase captures a sentiment that is felt across diverse situations, whether it's a small act of kindness in the face of a massive humanitarian crisis or a minor financial contribution to a colossal project.

Example Sentence

"While the charity's donation was generous, considering the magnitude of the problem they're addressing, it's just a drop in the ocean."

The idiom is a poignant reminder of scale and perspective. It doesn't necessarily devalue the "drop" but rather highlights the vastness of the "ocean" and the enormity of certain challenges or situations.

Barking Up the Wrong Tree

Meaning

The idiom "barking up the wrong tree" is used to convey that someone is pursuing a mistaken or misguided course of action or making a false assumption about something. Essentially, it suggests that one is directing their efforts inappropriately and will not get the desired results.

Origin

The idiom derives its meaning from a literal and easily visualized scenario:

1. Hunting and Treeing: The phrase has its roots in hunting practices. When hunting with dogs, especially with breeds trained to chase prey that climbs trees (like raccoons or squirrels), there could be instances where the dog would bark at the base of one tree, believing the prey was there, while the animal had actually escaped to a different tree. The dog, in its fervor, might continue barking, mistakenly thinking it has cornered its prey, when in reality, the prey is elsewhere.

2. 19th Century Usage: The idiom began to gain traction in American literature and discourse in the 19th century. It was a time when hunting, especially in rural areas, was a common pastime, making the metaphor easily relatable to many. Over time, the saying transitioned from its literal hunting origins to more metaphorical uses, symbolizing any misguided or misdirected efforts.

3. Evolution of the Phrase: While the hunting connection might be less obvious to modern urbanized audiences, the idiom's essence remains clear and has allowed it to endure in common speech. It effectively communicates the futility of incorrect assumptions or misguided endeavors.

Example Sentence

"He's trying to find out who played a prank on him by asking Sarah, but he's barking up the wrong tree; it was actually Mike who did it."

The idiom serves as a colorful way to warn or inform someone that they're off track or operating on a false premise. It's a gentle way of suggesting redirection or reevaluation of one's approach.

Hold Your Horses

The idiom "hold your horses" is a colloquial expression that means "wait a moment" or "be patient." It's often used to advise someone to slow down, think things through, or simply to pause before taking action.

Origin

The imagery behind this saying stems from a tangible and historically significant context:

1. Equestrian Roots: In its most literal sense, "hold your horses" would have been directed at someone controlling a team of horses, advising them to stop or keep the horses under control. Anyone who has ever tried to restrain a strong or eager horse would understand the challenge and the necessity of keeping the animal in check for safety.

2. 19th Century Usage: The phrase, as an idiom, began appearing in American print during the 19th century. It's worth noting that during this period, horses were a primary mode of transportation, and their handling was a part of daily life for many. Thus, the transition from a literal directive to a metaphorical expression emphasizing patience and caution was a natural evolution.

3. Further Historical Depth: Some sources suggest that similar admonitions, using different phrasing but related to horse reining, date back even further. The Bible's Book of Revelation (6:8) mentions "behold a pale horse," and while the wording is not the same, the idea of controlling or being wary of powerful forces (like horses) has deep historical roots.

Example Sentence

"Before you jump to conclusions about the situation, hold your horses and get all the facts."

In modern times, even with automobiles having long replaced horses as a primary means of transportation, the idiom endures. "Hold your horses" effectively communicates a universal sentiment: the importance of pausing, reflecting, and exercising patience. It resonates with the human tendency to sometimes act impulsively and the occasional need to be reminded to take a moment and assess before proceeding.

The Straw That Broke the Camel's Back

The idiom "the straw that broke the camel's back" refers to a seemingly minor or trivial action, situation, or incident that, when added to a series of previous burdens or problematic situations, causes a disproportionately large and negative reaction or consequence. It underscores the idea that there's a limit to endurance or patience, and while any one issue may seem minor in isolation, the cumulative effect can be overwhelming.

Origin

1. Weight and Capacity: Imagining a camel—a beast of burden known for its stamina and ability to carry heavy loads—being loaded with straw bit by bit makes the concept clear. Each piece of straw is light, but the accumulated weight can reach a tipping point where even a single extra straw can cause the camel's back to break.

2. Historical Usage: The exact origins of the idiom are somewhat murky, but it's believed to have roots in the 19th-century English lexicon. The full phrase "it is the last straw that breaks the camel's back" appeared in print in the 1870s, but similar sentiments, emphasizing the effect of cumulative burdens, can be found in literature and oral traditions predating this.

3. Variations: There are other versions of this expression across different cultures, emphasizing the same idea. For instance, in various countries, the metaphor might shift from camels and straw to horses and feathers or other combinations, but the core concept remains consistent.

Example Sentence

"After months of working long hours without any acknowledgment, the minor reprimand from his boss was the straw that broke the camel's back, and he decided to resign."

The idiom serves as a potent reminder that issues, no matter how trivial they seem in isolation, can accumulate over time, leading to significant consequences. It highlights the importance of being aware of cumulative stressors and burdens and understanding the broader context when seemingly small issues spark strong reactions.

Like Water off a Duck's Back

Meaning

The idiom "like water off a duck's back" describes a situation where something (often criticism or a negative comment) has no apparent effect on a person or is easily disregarded by them. When used in this context, it emphasizes the idea that the person is unaffected, indifferent, or resilient to the negative influence, just as water simply rolls off a duck's waterproof feathers without wetting it.

Origin

The phrase is rooted in a clear and observable natural phenomenon:

1. Nature of Duck Feathers: Ducks, and many other waterfowl, have specialized feathers coated with oils that repel water. This adaptation ensures that their feathers don't become waterlogged, allowing them to float and swim efficiently. When a duck emerges from the water, any droplets on its back or feathers simply roll off, leaving the bird relatively dry.

2. Early References: While it's challenging to pinpoint the first use of this idiom, its basis in the observable natural behavior of ducks likely made it a straightforward and relatable metaphor for many. The idiom has been in use for at least a few centuries, with variations of it appearing in 19th-century literature.

3. Universal Appeal: The visual simplicity and universality of watching water slide off a duck make this a compelling metaphor across cultures. The image is easy to conjure, and the message of resilience and unaffected demeanor is universally understood.

Example Sentence

"Every time I tell him that he needs to change his ways, it's like water off a duck's back – he just doesn't listen."

The idiom serves as a vivid depiction of resilience or indifference, depending on the context. It's a reminder that some people can remain unperturbed by criticism or negative influences, either due to their strength of character or sometimes due to ignorance or disregard.

Put All Your Eggs in One Basket

The idiom "put all your eggs in one basket" warns against concentrating all of one's resources, efforts, or hopes in a single venture or place. The underlying implication is that if something were to go wrong with that "basket," the person would lose everything, with no backup or alternative. The phrase is often used to advise diversifying one's investments, interests, or strategies to reduce risk.

Origin

1. Literal Interpretation: Imagine physically placing all of your eggs into one basket. If something were to happen to that basket—such as it being dropped or stolen—all the eggs would be lost. In contrast, if you spread your eggs across multiple baskets and one is compromised, you'd still have the eggs in the other baskets.

2. Historical Usage: The idiom's exact origins are hard to trace, but it's believed to have been a part of the English lexicon for centuries. One of the earliest recorded advisories against putting all one's eggs in one basket can be attributed to the novel "Don Quixote" by Miguel de Cervantes in the early 17th century. The advice was phrased slightly differently but conveyed the same cautionary message.

3. Widespread Recognition: Over time, this saying has been adopted, adapted, and recognized globally, often used in financial and strategic contexts. Its universality stems from the fundamental principle of risk management embedded within the phrase.

Example Sentence

"While investing in that startup might seem promising, it's wise not to put all your eggs in one basket and diversify your portfolio."

The idiom "put all your eggs in one basket" encapsulates a basic tenet of risk management and strategy: diversification. It's a caution against overcommitment to a single course of action or dependency on a singular outcome. The saying underscores the unpredictability of life and the inherent wisdom of spreading risk.

Eager Beaver

The idiom "eager beaver" describes a person who is extremely enthusiastic, hard-working, and zealous about a particular task or role. Such an individual often takes initiative, goes beyond what is required, and may sometimes be perceived as overly keen or diligent.

Origin

The term's vivid imagery draws from the well-documented behavior of a particular animal:

1. Nature of Beavers: Beavers are known for their industriousness. They are semiaquatic rodents that are famous for building dams, canals, and lodges. These dams, made of twigs, branches, and mud, are complex structures that serve as homes and protection against predators. The diligence and hard work displayed by beavers in constructing these intricate homes is a clear parallel to the industrious nature of an "eager" person.

2. Historical Usage: The term's association with keenness and enthusiasm likely originated from the observation of beavers' work ethic. While the exact origin of the phrase "eager beaver" in English is not well-documented, it appears to have gained popularity in the 20th century, particularly during and after World War II. It was used in the U.S. military to describe overly keen recruits or those who were enthusiastic to a fault.

3. Evolution of the Term: Over time, while the term can sometimes carry a slightly mocking or humorous undertone, suggesting someone is perhaps a little too keen for others' tastes, it's generally used in a positive manner to describe someone's enthusiasm and dedication.

Example Sentence

"Ever since she joined the team, Jenna has been such an eager beaver, always the first one in the office and the last one to leave."

The idiom "eager beaver" captures the essence of dedication and zeal. It paints a vivid picture of someone whose enthusiasm is akin to the relentless and industrious nature of beavers. Whether used in admiration of someone's work ethic or in jest about their over-enthusiasm, the phrase remains a colorful descriptor in the English language.

The Birds and the Bees

Meaning

"The birds and the bees" is a euphemistic idiom that refers to the way parents explain the basics of reproduction and human sexuality to their children. When someone says they had "the birds and the bees talk," they typically mean they received (or gave) a basic lesson on sexual education or where babies come from.

Origin

1. Nature's Example: Birds and bees both play roles in the process of pollination and reproduction in nature. Birds, especially certain species, engage in elaborate courtship dances and rituals to attract mates. Bees, on the other hand, transfer pollen from one flower to another, playing a critical role in plant reproduction.

2. Metaphorical Representation: Both processes can be viewed metaphorically in relation to human reproduction. The courting rituals of birds may symbolize attraction and mating in humans, while bees transferring pollen is analogous to the act of fertilization.

3. Literary Foundations: The exact phrase "birds and bees" isn't easily traceable to a single origin point, but the concept appears in literature going back centuries. For instance, the English poet Samuel Taylor Coleridge alluded to the idea in his work "Work Without Hope" (1825) when he wrote of "All nature seems at work ... The bees are stirring—birds are on the wing ... and I the while, the sole unbusy thing, not honey make, nor pair, nor build, nor sing."

4. Cultural Evolution: The idiom likely gained traction in the early 20th century as a delicate way for parents to broach the topic of reproduction with their children without having to delve into explicit details. Over time, it became a standard metaphor for this rite-of-passage conversation between parents and children.

Example Sentence

"When my son started asking where babies came from, I realized it was time for the birds and the bees talk."

"The birds and the bees" idiom encapsulates the cultural norms and sensitivities surrounding discussions of sexuality and reproduction. By using nature as a symbolic bridge, it offers a gentle introduction to a complex topic, providing a stepping stone for more detailed and nuanced conversations as one grows older.

Head in the Clouds

Having one's "head in the clouds" means being lost in daydreams or fantasies and being out of touch with reality. It describes a person who is perceived as absent-minded, overly imaginative, or not focused on the present situation. The idiom can imply a sense of aloofness, distraction, or impracticality.

Origin

The phrase draws upon the visual imagery of someone's head being elevated amongst the clouds, symbolizing distance from the grounded reality:

1. Clouds as Symbols: Clouds often represent abstraction, dreams, and loftiness. Since ancient times, looking up at the sky has been associated with daydreaming or pondering deeper, often abstract or philosophical, thoughts.

2. Historical Context: While the exact origins of the idiom aren't definitively documented, the concept has roots in ancient literature. Greek and Roman mythologies, for instance, feature gods and divine beings who reside in the sky or atop cloud-covered mountaintops, distant from the concerns of mere mortals.

3. Evolution over Time: Over the centuries, the imagery of someone being so lost in thought or fantasy that they seem to reside among the clouds became a popular metaphorical expression. By the 19th and 20th centuries, the idiom "head in the clouds" was commonly used in English literature and conversation to describe someone with a tendency to daydream or be lost in their thoughts.

Example Sentence

"While it's great that she's so creative and imaginative, sometimes she has her head in the clouds and forgets her daily responsibilities."

The idiom "head in the clouds" captures the essence of dreaminess versus practicality. It serves as a colorful way to describe someone's occasional disconnection from the immediate reality, suggesting both the beauty of imagination and the perils of neglecting the present. Whether used affectionately or critically, the phrase evokes a vivid image of dreamy detachment.

Can't See the Forest for the Trees

Meaning

The idiom "can't see the forest for the trees" describes a situation where someone is so focused on the details (represented by the "trees") that they fail to understand or perceive the larger situation, picture, or context (represented by the "forest"). In other words, they miss the broader implications or overarching theme because of an excessive concentration on individual elements.

Origin

1. Literal Interpretation: Imagine standing within a dense forest and being surrounded by numerous trees. If one only focuses on examining individual trees up close, they might not realize the vastness or overall layout of the entire forest.

2. Historical Usage: The concept behind the phrase has been present for centuries, emphasizing the balance between the macro and the micro, or the general and the specific. One of the earliest recorded uses in English literature is from John Heywood's 1546 proverb collection, where he wrote, "You cannot see the wood for the trees." Over time, "wood" became "forest" in the more commonly used versions of the idiom, especially in American English.

3. Philosophical Implications: The idiom touches on a recurring theme in philosophy and contemplation: the tension between particulars and universals. The saying is a reminder of the need to step back and see the broader perspective, especially when one becomes mired in details.

Example Sentence

"While the committee has been debating on the color of the binder for hours, they can't see the forest for the trees and realize that what's inside the binder is what truly matters."

The idiom "can't see the forest for the trees" serves as a metaphorical caution against becoming overly detail-oriented at the expense of understanding the bigger picture. It emphasizes the importance of perspective and holistic understanding in various contexts, from daily tasks to grander philosophical ideas.

Take the Bull by the Horns

The idiom "take the bull by the horns" means to confront a difficult or challenging situation head-on and with determined courage. It suggests addressing a problem directly rather than avoiding it or being passive.

Origin

The vivid imagery of this idiom draws upon the risky act of grabbing a bull directly by its horns:

1. Bullfighting and Rodeos: The origin likely stems from the world of bullfighting or rodeos. In both these events, bulls are known to be dangerous and unpredictable animals. The act of grabbing a bull by its horns would be a direct and fearless way to confront and control it, though incredibly risky. This action would demonstrate courage, assertiveness, and direct confrontation, which is how the idiom is metaphorically applied to other situations.

2. Historical Usage: While the precise origin in terms of time and place isn't definitively known, the phrase has been used in English since at least the 18th century to describe confronting challenges directly. Its usage in literature and culture has solidified its Meaning over time.

3. Symbolism of the Bull: In many cultures, the bull is a symbol of strength, stubbornness, and potential danger. The act of taking control over such a powerful creature by its horns paints a clear picture of bravery and direct action.

Example Sentence

"Instead of complaining about the problems in his department, Jake decided to take the bull by the horns and proposed comprehensive solutions to the team."

The idiom "take the bull by the horns" encapsulates a proactive approach to life's challenges. It suggests not just facing problems but actively seeking to address and overcome them. In using this phrase, speakers often encourage a bold, fearless stance in the face of adversity or challenges.

A Bird in the Hand is Worth Two in the Bush

Meaning

The idiom "a bird in the hand is worth two in the bush" conveys that it's better to have a certain advantage or a sure thing than the mere potential of a greater one. Essentially, it advises valuing what you already possess over what you might get but is not guaranteed.

Origin

This idiom, rooted in ancient wisdom, merges practicality with the unpredictable nature of ambition:

1. Hunting and Gathering: The phrase might have originated from ancient hunting practices. A bird in one's hand, caught and secured, is a guaranteed meal. Meanwhile, seeing two birds in a bush might be promising, but they could easily fly away, leaving the hunter with nothing.

2. Ancient Texts: The sentiment, if not the exact phrasing, appears in texts from various cultures over millennia. One of the earliest versions is found in the Greek text of Aesop's Fables, dating back to the 6th century BCE. The idiom as we know it now, however, was first recorded in English in the 15th century. It's included in John Capgrave's "The Life of Saint Katharine" from 1450.

3. Adapting the Phrase: The exact wording has varied over time. Early iterations in English were closer to "better one bird in hand than ten in the woods." The modern version of the idiom was popularized by the 16th century and has remained consistent since then.

Example Sentence

"Even though the new job offer might pay a bit more, I'd be starting from scratch and leaving my senior position here. After all, a bird in the hand is worth two in the bush."

The idiom "a bird in the hand is worth two in the bush" serves as a cautionary reminder about the risks of greed or overreaching. It emphasizes the value of certainty and contentment, suggesting that chasing after uncertain prospects might result in losing what one already has. In a broader philosophical context, it touches upon themes of gratitude, contentment, and the human tendency to undervalue present blessings in favor of future possibilities.

Raining Cats and Dogs

Meaning

The idiom "raining cats and dogs" is used to describe a very heavy downpour or intense rainstorm. It doesn't literally mean animals are falling from the sky but rather emphasizes the intensity and ferocity of the rainfall.

Origin

The exact origins of this peculiar phrase are unclear, and numerous theories attempt to explain its etymology:

1. Old English Phrases: Some believe the phrase could be derived from old English phrases where "cat" and "dog" were used to describe heavy rain and strong winds, respectively, though solid evidence is lacking.

2. Medieval Living Conditions: One of the more popular theories suggests that during heavy rainfalls in medieval European towns, the streets would often become torrents of rushing water. Considering the poor drainage systems and the thatched roofs where animals might seek refuge, it's speculated that these creatures (like cats and small dogs) could be washed out, giving an appearance of "raining" animals.

3. Norse Mythology: Another theory connects the phrase to Norse mythology, where cats were associated with heavy rains and dogs (often accompanying Odin, the storm god) symbolized wind.

4. Greek Expression: The Greeks believed that cats could influence the weather, especially rain. Dogs, being sacred to Hecate, were associated with the stormy aspects of weather. A juxtaposition of these beliefs might have led to an early version of the phrase.

5. Literal Interpretations: Some even say the idiom derives from actual incidents where small animals got swept up by tornadoes or similar weather phenomena and then rained down elsewhere, although this is more speculative and less likely as an origin.

Example Sentence

"I forgot my umbrella at home, and it's raining cats and dogs outside! I'll be drenched if I step out now."

The idiom "raining cats and dogs" captures the imaginative and colorful nature of language. While its exact origin remains shrouded in mystery, the phrase has endured through centuries, standing as a testament to the dynamic and vivid nature of idiomatic expressions. It reminds us of a time when such phrases were crafted from daily observations, myths, beliefs, and the confluence of cultures.

Emotions & Feelings

Walking on Air

The idiom "walking on air" describes a feeling of extreme happiness or elation. Someone who is "walking on air" is so joyful that they feel as if they're floating or as light as air, free from all worries or concerns.

Origin

1. Physical Elation: The sensation of lightness or floating is often associated with feelings of joy or happiness. Just as heavy feelings or "a weight on one's shoulders" is used to describe sadness or burden, the opposite sensation of weightlessness is used to depict happiness.

2. Literary Usage: The phrase has been used in literature and poetry to describe a state of bliss or elation. Classic literature, including works by authors like William Wordsworth, has used similar imagery to capture the ethereal nature of joy.

3. Connection to Dreams and Aspirations: The idea of floating or flying often appears in dream interpretations as a symbol of freedom, success, or achieving one's goals. This could have influenced the idiom's connection to feelings of joy and accomplishment.

4. Evolution Over Time: It's possible the phrase evolved from similar expressions that describe feelings of happiness using the imagery of lightness or elevation. Over time, "walking on air" might have become popularized and entered common parlance.

Example Sentence

"After receiving the news of her promotion, Maria felt like she was walking on air for the rest of the day."

The idiom "walking on air" beautifully encapsulates the weightless, soaring feeling that accompanies moments of pure joy. It's a reminder of those instances in life where happiness is so profound that it feels as if the laws of physics no longer apply, and one is simply floating above the ground, unburdened by life's usual worries.

Cry Over Spilled Milk

Meaning

The idiom "cry over spilled milk" means to waste time feeling upset about a minor disappointment or something that has already happened and cannot be changed. It suggests that it's pointless to lament over things that are out of one's control.

Origin

While the imagery of spilled milk is straightforward, the historical context adds depth:

1. Medieval Proverbs: The phrase's sentiment can be traced back to ancient cultures. There are sayings in James Howell's "Proverbs" in 1659 that convey a similar idea, although not directly mentioning milk: "No weeping for shed milk." The transition to the phrase we're familiar with today evolved over time.

2. Literal Interpretation: In agrarian societies, spilling milk could be seen as a genuine loss, especially if resources were scarce. Dairy was a valuable commodity. However, once milk has been spilled, no amount of regret can retrieve it, hence highlighting the futility of regret over past mistakes.

3. Popular Usage: The modern version, "It's no use crying over spilled milk," came into frequent use in the 19th century and was popularized in various literary works.

Example Sentence

"I know you're disappointed you didn't win, but it's no use crying over spilled milk. Let's prepare for the next competition."

The idiom "cry over spilled milk" encapsulates a universal piece of wisdom: the importance of moving forward and not getting bogged down by past mistakes or disappointments. It's a call to action, encouraging resilience, acceptance, and a forward-facing attitude. This timeless advice, wrapped up in the simple imagery of a dairy mishap, resonates across cultures and ages, reminding us that some things, once done, cannot be undone, and it's more productive to look to the future than dwell on the past.

Have a Chip on One's Shoulder

To "have a chip on one's shoulder" refers to someone holding a grudge or grievance, often stemming from a past wrong or perceived slight. It also implies that the person is carrying an attitude of defiant or combative pride, constantly looking for an opportunity to prove themselves or settle a score.

Origin

The origin of this idiom is quite colorful and rooted in historical practices:

1. Wooden Chips and Challenges: One widely accepted origin dates back to the early 19th-century practices in the United States. Young men looking to prove their toughness would place a wood chip on their shoulder, daring anyone to knock it off, thus initiating a fight. If someone accepted the challenge, they'd knock off the chip, and a brawl would ensue.

2. Dockyard Disputes: Another theory links the idiom to the 19th-century shipyards of North America. When workers had disputes or grievances about pay or conditions, they'd display this by placing a chip of wood on their shoulder and challenging their employer or foreman to knock it off, signifying their readiness for a physical confrontation over the issue.

3. Literary References: The phrase started appearing in literature in the mid-19th century, solidifying its place in the English lexicon. By the latter part of the century, the idiom was widely understood to mean harboring a grievance.

Example Sentence

"Ever since he was passed over for the promotion, Mike has had a chip on his shoulder, always looking for an argument with the management."

The idiom "have a chip on one's shoulder" embodies the human tendency to harbor resentment and the desire to confront or prove oneself when feeling slighted or undervalued. Over time, the idiom has evolved from its combative origins to symbolize any unresolved grievance or resentment, whether it leads to confrontation or not. It serves as a vivid metaphorical reminder of the weight and burden of holding onto grudges.

Wear One's Heart on One's Sleeve

To "wear one's heart on one's sleeve" means to openly display one's emotions or feelings, rather than keeping them hidden. Someone who does this doesn't hide their emotions, making it easy for others to discern how they feel about something. It's often associated with sincerity, vulnerability, and a lack of pretense.

Origin

1. Shakespearean Roots: One of the most widely accepted origins of the phrase is from William Shakespeare's play "Othello," written in 1604. The character Iago says: "For when my outward action doth demonstrate/The native act and figure of my heart/In complement extern, 'tis not long after/But I will wear my heart upon my sleeve/For daws to peck at: I am not what I am." Here, Iago discusses his deceitful nature, indicating that if he were to display his true intentions (wear his heart on his sleeve), it would leave him vulnerable to attacks (by daws or birds).

2. Medieval Traditions: Another theory, albeit less substantiated, ties the idiom to medieval jousting traditions. Knights would wear tokens from their ladies, often tied to their arms, as symbols of their affection and dedication. This public display could be seen as them literally wearing their emotions (or heart) on their sleeves.

3. Literal Interpretation: The heart has long been considered the symbolic center of emotion and passion. Displaying it on one's sleeve, an external and visible part of clothing, represents the act of showing one's deepest emotions to the world.

Example Sentence

"Sarah always wears her heart on her sleeve; you can tell exactly how she feels by the look on her face."

The idiom "wear one's heart on one's sleeve" captures the vulnerability and sincerity of unabashed emotional expression. It speaks to the human experience of emotion and the choices individuals make about expressing or concealing their feelings. In a world where pretense and facade can be common, the phrase celebrates genuine, unfiltered emotion, even with the risks that such transparency might entail.

Bite the Bullet

To "bite the bullet" means to face a difficult or unpleasant situation with courage and determination. It suggests confronting a challenge head-on, even if it's something one would rather avoid.

Origin

The historical background of this idiom provides a visceral image of its meaning:

1. Military Origins: The most widely accepted origin of this phrase dates back to the days before anesthesia was commonly used in medical procedures. During battles, soldiers with severe injuries would often have to undergo field surgeries or amputations. To help them endure the pain, they were given a lead musket ball (a bullet) to bite on. Biting on something hard could distract from the pain, help prevent the person from biting their tongue, and reduce the likelihood of them screaming.

2. Indian Rebellion: Another recorded instance comes from the time of the Indian Rebellion of 1857. Rudyard Kipling's works from the late 19th century make reference to the practice, suggesting soldiers "bit the bullet" during surgical procedures.

3. Shift in Usage: While the original context was literal, the transition to its metaphorical use reflects the courage and stoicism soldiers displayed in those dire circumstances. Over time, it came to symbolize facing any challenging or daunting situation with bravery.

Example Sentence

"I know the upcoming meeting with the client will be tough, but it's time to bite the bullet and address their concerns."

The idiom "bite the bullet" draws a powerful parallel between the sheer physical courage soldiers once displayed on the battlefield and the mental or emotional strength required to face challenging situations in our daily lives. It's a vivid reminder of the human capacity for resilience and bravery, even in the face of adversity. The phrase encourages a bold confrontation with obstacles, suggesting that, like soldiers of the past, we too can endure and overcome.

Butterflies in One's Stomach

To have "butterflies in one's stomach" means to feel nervous, anxious, or excited, usually in anticipation of something that's about to happen. The sensation is likened to having fluttering butterflies moving around in one's belly.

Origin

1. Bodily Response: When humans feel nervous or anxious, the body releases adrenaline. This stress response diverts blood away from non-essential functions, like digestion, to prepare for a "fight or flight" reaction. The decreased blood flow in the stomach can cause a fluttering sensation, similar to that of fluttering wings.

2. Ancient Associations: While the exact origin of the phrase is somewhat unclear, the association between the stomach and emotions goes back to ancient times. Many cultures believed that emotions, especially love and anxiety, originated in the stomach. This belief might be tied to the noticeable sensations the stomach exhibits when one experiences strong feelings.

3. Modern Usage: The phrase's modern form and widespread usage in the English language seems to have developed in the 20th century. The imagery of light, fluttering butterflies effectively captures the subtle, fluttery sensations of anxiety or excitement one might feel.

Example Sentence

"Every time I have to speak in public, I get butterflies in my stomach."

The idiom "butterflies in one's stomach" paints a vivid picture of human emotion, encapsulating the physical sensations of anticipation and anxiety. It's a universally relatable phrase, as most people have felt this mix of excitement and nervousness at pivotal moments in their lives, whether before a performance, during a significant life event, or in the throes of early romantic feelings. The choice of the butterfly, a delicate and light creature, underscores the gentle, fluttering nature of the sensation, making the experience something tender and inherently human.

Jump for Joy

To "jump for joy" means to express one's happiness or excitement in an exuberant manner. It signifies a feeling of elation so strong that it propels one into a physical, jubilant action, such as jumping.

Origin

The roots of this idiom are both literal and deeply rooted in human expression:

1. Natural Human Expression: Jumping or leaping as an expression of joy or excitement is a universal human behavior. Across cultures and throughout history, people have often leaped into the air or danced to physically express strong positive emotions. This is not limited to humans either; many animals also exhibit jumping behaviors when excited or playful.

2. Biblical References: The concept of jumping for joy can be traced back to religious texts, most notably the Bible. There are passages where individuals and groups are described as leaping or jumping in expressions of religious ecstasy or joy. For instance, in the Book of Luke 6:23, it's written: "Rejoice in that day and leap for joy, because great is your reward in heaven."

3. Literary Legacy: As with many idioms, literature has played a significant role in popularizing and preserving the phrase. Over time, "jump for joy" has been used in poetry, plays, and novels to evoke strong feelings of happiness or elation.

Example Sentence

"When she received the news of her promotion, she wanted to jump for joy."

The idiom "jump for joy" captures the sheer physicality of human emotion. It's a reminder of how intense feelings, especially positive ones, can manifest in our actions, leading us to express our emotions in outwardly demonstrative ways. The idiom touches on a shared human experience, where happiness and excitement are so overwhelming that they break free from the confines of the heart and mind, leading to spontaneous, joyful movements.

A Weight Off One's Shoulders

Meaning

To have "a weight off one's shoulders" means to feel relieved after being freed from a burden or worry that one has been carrying for some time. It signifies the alleviation of a stressor or responsibility that has been causing distress or concern.

Origin

1. Physical Burden Representation: The act of carrying weight, especially on one's back or shoulders, has long been associated with bearing responsibilities or burdens. Just as a physical weight can tire or strain a person, emotional or mental burdens can also be exhausting.

2. Antiquity and Middle Ages: The concept of burdens, both literal and figurative, has been explored throughout history. For instance, in ancient civilizations, manual labor, like carrying heavy loads, was a common task, making the shoulder's weight a real and relatable concept. In medieval literature and religious texts, the image of carrying a weight often symbolized trials, tribulations, or sins. One notable example is Christian's journey in John Bunyan's "The Pilgrim's Progress," where the protagonist carries the weight of his sins on his back until he's able to find relief.

3. Transition to Metaphorical Use: Over time, as societies evolved and many burdens became less about physical weight and more about mental or emotional stress, the idiom transitioned to more frequently denote intangible worries or responsibilities. The relief of such burdens, then, became akin to setting down a heavy weight one had been carrying.

Example Sentence

"After months of uncertainty, getting the job offer was like a weight off his shoulders."

The idiom "a weight off one's shoulders" beautifully captures the physical and emotional crossover of human experience. The sense of relief, whether from physical labor or mental stress, is a universal feeling. This phrase underscores the intimate relationship between the body and the mind, reminding us that emotional or mental challenges can be as taxing as any physical weight we might bear. In its essence, it speaks to the human desire for relief, comfort, and the moments of respite we all seek from life's many burdens.

Blow Off Steam

To "blow off steam" means to release pent-up energy or emotion, often by engaging in a physical activity or by expressing oneself. It signifies a way of relieving stress, frustration, or anger in order to avoid potential negative consequences or overreactions.

Origin

The idiom finds its roots in the industrial era and the workings of steam engines:

1. Steam Engines and Safety Valves: In the 18th and 19th centuries, steam engines played a crucial role in the Industrial Revolution. These engines operated by boiling water to produce steam, which then drove mechanical processes. If the pressure inside the engine built up too much without a release, it could cause the engine to explode. To prevent this, steam engines were equipped with safety valves that allowed excess steam to be released, or "blown off," ensuring the machine's smooth and safe operation.

2. Metaphorical Transition: Given the dangers of excess pressure in steam engines, the act of releasing steam became synonymous with averting a potential crisis. Translating this to human emotions, where pent-up feelings can similarly lead to explosive reactions, the phrase "blow off steam" came to symbolize the release of emotional or psychological pressure.

3. Modern Usage: In today's parlance, the idiom has expanded beyond its industrial roots, widely used to describe various methods people employ to relax or release tension, whether that's through physical activity, talking, or other outlets.

Example Sentence

"After a stressful week at work, she went for a long run to blow off steam."

The idiom "blow off steam" ties our emotional well-being to the intricate mechanics of industrial machinery. It highlights the importance of self-regulation and the need for outlets to cope with the pressures of daily life. Just as steam engines needed a mechanism to release pressure and ensure safety, humans also require ways to manage their emotions, emphasizing the need for balance and self-awareness in both machinery and the human psyche.

In High Spirits

To be "in high spirits" means to be cheerful, lively, and in a good mood. It signifies a state of positivity, enthusiasm, or general happiness.

Origin

The phrase "in high spirits" has an etymology deeply connected with the way emotions and mood have been historically understood:

1. Historical Understanding of Spirits: In ancient and medieval times, various cultures believed that human emotions and behaviors were influenced by "spirits" or "humors." For instance, the Greeks posited the existence of four humors: blood, yellow bile, black bile, and phlegm, each corresponding to a particular temperament or mood.

2. Elevation as a Positive Descriptor: Throughout history, things that are elevated or "high" have often been associated with positive attributes or esteemed states of being. For example, in religious contexts, the heavens or the skies are often seen as places of happiness, purity, or divinity. Similarly, in daily language, being "on top of the world" or "over the moon" suggests elation or joy.

3. Transition to Modern Use: As language evolved, the term "spirits" began to be used more broadly to refer to one's mood or emotional state, decoupled from its ancient roots in humor theory. Thus, to be "in high spirits" combined the positive connotation of elevation with the idea of a buoyant or joyful mood.

Example Sentence

"Despite the rainy weather, the team remained in high spirits, laughing and sharing stories."

The idiom "in high spirits" encapsulates the ebbs and flows of human emotion. Its roots delve deep into history, reflecting how humanity has long sought to understand and articulate the nuances of mood and temperament. Today, the phrase remains a vibrant testament to the resilience of the human spirit, invoking images of joy, hope, and positivity even in the face of challenges. It reminds us of the universal human capacity for happiness and the ways in which we uplift ourselves and others.

Down in the Dumps

Meaning

To be "down in the dumps" means to be unhappy, dejected, or in a state of low spirits. The idiom conveys feelings of sadness, despondency, or melancholy.

Origin

Tracing the precise origins of idioms can often be challenging due to their colloquial nature and evolution over time. "Down in the dumps" is no exception, with a history that is both intriguing and somewhat speculative:

1. Medieval Reference: The earliest known use of the word "dumps" in English literature to denote a state of melancholy comes from Sir Thomas Malory's "Le Morte d'Arthur" in the 15th century. Here, "dumps" referred to a sorrowful tune or lament. Over time, the word began to represent not just the music but also the mood it evoked.

2. Possible Association with Dumpsites: There's some speculation, though not definitively proven, that the modern interpretation of the idiom might have been influenced by the idea of a "dump" as a place for discarded waste or garbage. Such places are often viewed as undesirable or depressing. However, this connection is more associative than directly etymological.

3. Evolution of Usage: As language evolved, the phrase "in the dumps" or "down in the dumps" became more popularly used to describe someone who looked or felt downcast or unhappy. The added "down" in the idiom intensifies the feeling of being low or sad, making the entire phrase a vivid descriptor of despondency.

Example Sentence

"After hearing the unfortunate news, she's been down in the dumps all week."

The idiom "down in the dumps" paints a poignant picture of the human experience of sadness. Its usage over centuries is a testament to the universality of such feelings and the human need to articulate them. While its exact origins may remain shrouded in mystery, its ability to capture the essence of melancholy in just a few words remains undiminished. It serves as a gentle reminder that everyone, at some point, has their moments of feeling low, and in recognizing and naming these feelings, we take the first steps towards empathy and understanding.

Burst One's Bubble

Meaning

To "burst one's bubble" means to dispel someone's illusions, shatter their idealistic beliefs, or bring them back to reality by presenting facts or the truth. It typically refers to destroying a comforting, yet often mistaken, belief or ideal.

Origin

The imagery and origins of the phrase are rooted in the transient and delicate nature of bubbles:

1. Nature of Bubbles: Bubbles, whether blown from soap or formed in liquids, are fragile, transient, and easily burst. Their beautiful, reflective surfaces are enchanting to observe, but they are ephemeral and can be destroyed by even the slightest touch or gust of wind.

2. Metaphorical Extension: Drawing from the physical properties of bubbles, the phrase began to symbolize the fragile nature of dreams, illusions, or misconceptions. Just as a bubble can be easily popped, returning it to its unremarkable liquid state, a person's illusions or mistaken beliefs can be "burst" when confronted with reality.

3. Usage over Time: While it's challenging to pinpoint the exact first use of this idiom, its imagery and the experience it denotes are universal. Over time, the phrase has been ingrained into the English language as a colorful way to describe the sometimes harsh collision between idealistic beliefs and stark reality.

Example Sentence

"She always believed that her favorite celebrity could do no wrong, but the recent news articles seemed to burst her bubble."

The idiom "burst one's bubble" poignantly captures the intersection of hope, illusion, and reality. In its essence, it's a phrase that underscores the human tendency to hold onto beliefs or perceptions, sometimes against overwhelming evidence to the contrary. It reminds us of the delicate balance between optimism and realism, between seeing the world as we wish it to be and accepting it as it truly is. While the act of "bursting someone's bubble" might seem harsh, it often represents a necessary return to reality, fostering growth and a deeper understanding of the world around us.

Lose One's Temper

To "lose one's temper" means to suddenly become very angry or upset, typically resulting in an emotional outburst. It suggests a loss of control over one's emotions, especially anger or frustration.

Origin

1. Temper as Balance: Historically, the word "temper" was used to describe a middle state or balanced condition, especially pertaining to the blending of different elements or substances to achieve a desired consistency or quality. For example, in metallurgy, tempering refers to the process of heating and cooling metal to achieve a balance of hardness and elasticity.

2. Temper as Emotional Balance: Over time, the term "temper" began to be associated with not just physical but also emotional balance. It referred to a calm and balanced state of mind, free from extreme emotions. In this context, to "lose one's temper" meant to deviate from this balanced emotional state, especially towards anger.

3. Evolution of the Idiom: As language and culture evolved, the association of "temper" with anger became more prominent. While temper can still mean disposition or temperament in general, in the context of this idiom, it is almost exclusively associated with anger.

Example Sentence

"He was usually calm and collected, but when he found out his work had been discarded, he lost his temper."

The idiom "lose one's temper" reflects the human struggle to maintain emotional balance and composure. Its origin links our emotional states with the intricate processes of crafting materials, drawing a parallel between the balance sought in both realms. The phrase serves as a reminder of the volatile nature of emotions, and how, just as metals might need repeated tempering to achieve the right balance, humans too need self-awareness and self-regulation to maintain emotional equilibrium. In highlighting the momentary lapses where this balance is lost, the idiom underscores the importance of emotional intelligence in navigating interpersonal interactions and life's challenges.

Over the Moon

Meaning

To be "over the moon" means to be extremely happy, delighted, or thrilled about something. It implies a level of joy that feels almost otherworldly or ecstatic.

Origin

The origins and evolution of the phrase are intertwined with cultural and literary references:

1. Lunar Fascination: The moon, as a celestial object, has always captured human imagination and emotion. Throughout history, it's been a symbol of wonder, mystery, and romance. Being "over" such a magnificent object would suggest a state of heightened emotion or elation.

2. Literary Roots: One of the earliest known associations of extreme happiness with the moon can be traced back to the nursery rhyme "Hey Diddle Diddle," where "the cow jumped over the moon." The fantastical imagery of a cow leaping over the moon paints a picture of jubilation and wonder.

3. Evolution in Pop Culture: The phrase gradually made its way into broader English vernacular, especially during the 20th century. It gained traction in pop culture, perhaps even more so during the space race era, when the idea of literally going "over the moon" became a real, tangible achievement.

Example Sentence

"When she received the news of her promotion, she was over the moon."

The idiom "over the moon" beautifully encapsulates the peaks of human emotion. Drawing from age-old lunar symbolism and integrating it with feelings of exuberance, the phrase creates a vivid portrayal of joy that's almost transcendental in nature. In expressing happiness as being "over the moon," the idiom reminds us of those rare, delightful moments in life when joy feels boundless, uncontainable, and as vast as the night sky. It's a testament to the human spirit's capacity for delight, celebrating those moments when we feel on top of the world—or, in this case, the moon.

Cost an Arm and a Leg

If something "costs an arm and a leg," it means it is very expensive or overly pricey. The idiom emphasizes the idea that the cost of an item or experience is so high that one would have to sacrifice a great deal to obtain it.

Origin

1. Historical Art and Portraiture: One theory posits that the phrase has origins in 18th-century portraiture. Painters would charge more for larger paintings and the price would increase based on the number of limbs (arms or legs) that were to be painted. Painting limbs required greater skill and detail. However, this theory, while intriguing, is not heavily substantiated with concrete evidence.

2. World War II and Sacrifice: A more widely accepted origin traces the phrase back to the World War II era. Soldiers, risking their lives and limbs, paid a high price for their involvement. References to the loss of an "arm and a leg" in the war began to appear in newspapers and literature during and after the war, highlighting the high cost of conflict.

3. Evolution of the Phrase: By the late 1940s and 1950s, the phrase started being used more generally in the U.S. to describe anything that was considered expensive, and not just about literal sacrifice. It captured the sentiment of something costing a prohibitive amount.

Example Sentence

"I'd love to buy that designer dress, but it costs an arm and a leg."

The idiom "cost an arm and a leg" offers a vivid illustration of the lengths to which one might have to go, or the sacrifices one might have to make, to procure something. While its precise origins remain debated, the emotional weight and emphasis of the phrase are clear: it's a commentary on the steep price of desires and aspirations, be they material, experiential, or even more profound. By likening the cost of something to the loss of vital body parts, the idiom accentuates the value, sacrifice, and sometimes the extremes of human pursuit. Whether used in jest about an expensive item or more somberly to reflect on deeper sacrifices, the phrase remains a poignant reminder of the costs and values we assign in life.

At One's Wit's End

To be "at one's wit's end" means to be so perplexed or frustrated that one is unsure of what to do next. It denotes a state of extreme confusion or desperation, where an individual feels they have exhausted all their ideas or options and don't know how to proceed.

Origin

1. Biblical Origins: The phrase can be traced back to the Bible. Specifically, it appears in the King James Version in Psalms 107:27: "They reel to and fro, and stagger like a drunken man, and are at their wits' end." Here, it describes sailors in distress at sea, facing storms and massive waves, uncertain of their survival.

2. Middle English and the Concept of 'Wits': In Middle English, the term "wits" didn't just refer to humor or cleverness as it might today. Instead, "wits" referred more broadly to one's mental faculties or intelligence. This usage dates back to Old English and implies one's ability to think, reason, and understand. To be at the "end" of one's wits, then, means to have exhausted all one's cognitive resources or strategies.

3. Evolution Over Time: Over centuries, the phrase evolved from its biblical use to become a more general expression. It was utilized in various works of literature and eventually became a well-known idiom in the English language.

Example Sentence

"After trying every possible solution to fix the computer glitch, Jane was at her wit's end."

The idiom "at one's wit's end" captures the essence of human vulnerability when faced with insurmountable challenges or confounding situations. It's a declaration of one's limitations, an admission that they've reached the boundary of their understanding or patience. In a world where answers are often expected quickly and solutions are anticipated to be at one's fingertips, this phrase resonates deeply, acknowledging the universality of moments where we simply don't have the answers. It serves as a humble reminder that despite our vast capabilities, there are instances where solutions evade us, and challenges test the limits of our cognition and resolve.

Close to the Chest (or Close to the Vest)

To keep something "close to the chest" or "close to the vest" means to keep one's intentions, plans, or information secret or private. It indicates a sense of caution and discretion, not revealing one's cards or intentions to others.

Origin

1. Card Games: This idiom finds its roots in the world of card games. In many card games, players are dealt a hand that they do not reveal to their opponents. Keeping one's cards "close to the vest" or "close to the chest" ensures that other players cannot catch a glimpse of your cards, hence not revealing any potential strategy. The closer the cards are held to the body, the less visible they are to other players, ensuring that they can't anticipate your next move.

2. Vests and Attire: The variation between "vest" and "chest" in the idiom can be attributed to different cultural or regional uses. Vests, being a more common article of clothing in some regions, led to the term "close to the vest," whereas in other regions where the focus was more on the body part than the attire, "close to the chest" became prevalent.

3. Wider Usage: Over time, this tactical approach in card games transcended its original context. The phrase began to be applied to any situation where discretion and secrecy were beneficial, be it in business negotiations, strategic planning, or personal matters.

Example Sentence

"Even though everyone was curious about the company's next move, the CEO kept his plans close to the chest until the official announcement."

The idiom "close to the chest" or "close to the vest" beautifully encapsulates the notion of strategic discretion. It paints a vivid picture of the guardedness and prudence one employs, much like a card player unsure of the game's outcome. In life, as in games, revealing too much can sometimes be a disadvantage. Whether it's a businessperson strategizing their next move, a writer holding back a plot twist, or an individual protecting personal news, this idiom resonates with moments of restraint and careful strategy. It's a nod to the gamesmanship inherent in various aspects of life and the judicious balance of transparency and secrecy.

Get Cold Feet

Meaning

To "get cold feet" means to become apprehensive or hesitant about doing something, particularly at the last minute. It is often used in the context of backing out of a commitment or decision due to a sudden onset of fear or doubt.

Origin

1. Military Theories: One theory posits that the phrase originated in the military realm. Soldiers who got cold feet during wartime might have been unable or unwilling to move, possibly due to the freezing conditions of the trenches during the world wars. Their immobility was then likened to fear or hesitation.

2. Theatrical Usage: Another origin story traces back to the 19th century in the theatrical world. It was believed that nervous performers waiting in the wings got cold feet due to poor circulation brought on by anxiety.

3. German Proverb: The phrase might also have roots in a German proverb. The German expression "kalte Füße bekommen" directly translates to "get cold feet" and means to get scared and try to run away. It's believed that this proverb was translated and integrated into English, capturing a similar sentiment.

4. Literary References: The earliest recorded use in English appears in the 1890s. Stephen Crane, in his book "Maggie: A Girl of the Streets" (1893), wrote: "I knew this was the way it would be. They got cold feet."

Example Sentence

"She was excited about skydiving but got cold feet just before the jump."

The idiom "get cold feet" evokes a vivid imagery of the physical sensation one might feel when overwhelmed by nerves—like feet turning cold due to circulatory changes when anxious. This phrase taps into the universal experience of doubt, especially in the face of significant decisions or life-changing events. Whether it's the bride or groom hesitating before saying "I do," an investor reconsidering a large financial gamble, or a performer anxious before taking the stage, "getting cold feet" captures the momentary lapse of confidence that every individual, no matter how brave or decisive, can occasionally face. It's a reminder of the shared human vulnerability that comes with stepping into the unknown.

Tug at One's Heartstrings

To "tug at one's heartstrings" means to evoke strong feelings of sympathy, compassion, or sentimentality in someone. It signifies a deep emotional response, often elicited by a poignant scene, story, or situation.

Origin

1. Musical Imagery: The term "heartstrings" dates back to the late 15th century and originally referred to the tendons that were believed to brace the heart. These tendons or "chords" were imagined to function much like the strings of musical instruments. Just as the strings of a musical instrument, when plucked or strummed, produce resonant sounds, the heartstrings, when metaphorically "tugged" or "plucked," would result in deep emotional feelings or responses.

2. Anatomical References: The term "heartstrings" is also a poetic transformation of the actual strings or tendons in the heart, known as chordae tendineae. These are string-like bands of tissue that connect the papillary muscles to the tricuspid and mitral valves in the heart. While they have no relation to feelings or emotions, the poetic idea of the heart being the center of emotion and these "strings" being tied to one's feelings is evocative and became symbolic over time.

3. Literary Usage: The term "heartstrings" in a figurative sense, implying deep emotion, appears in various literary works over centuries, reinforcing the heart's connection to feelings. One such reference is in Shakespeare's play "Richard III," where the term is used in Act 1, Scene 1: "You have no cause to hold my friendship doubtful; I never was nor never will be false."

Example Sentence

"The documentary about the orphaned children tugged at everyone's heartstrings, moving many to tears."

The idiom "tug at one's heartstrings" paints a beautifully vivid picture of our emotional vulnerabilities. The metaphor of the heart, which is often seen as the seat of emotions in many cultures, being connected to strings that can be pulled to produce feelings is both poignant and evocative. Whether it's a touching scene in a movie, a heartfelt story of loss and love, or witnessing a kind act, the moments that "tug at our heartstrings" are the ones that remind us of our shared humanity, our capacities for empathy and compassion, and the deep connections that bind us all. Such moments underscore the profound emotional depths that we, as humans, are capable of experiencing.

Burn the Candle at Both Ends

Meaning

To "burn the candle at both ends" means to exhaust oneself by doing too much, especially by working late into the night and beginning again early in the morning. In essence, it connotes overworking or trying to do too much at once, often at the cost of one's health or well-being.

Origin

1. Literal Usage: In a very literal sense, if one were to light a candle at both ends, it would burn out twice as quickly. While it might provide more light for a short duration, it's unsustainable and will leave you in the dark sooner. This imagery captured the essence of overexertion and its potential consequences.

2. 17th Century References: The concept, if not the exact phrase, was used in the 17th century. The French expression, "brûler la chandelle par les deux bouts," translates directly to burning the candle at both ends and means to live extravagantly. Over time, this meaning evolved to not just spending resources but also one's energy.

3. 20th Century Popularization: The exact phrase as we know it became popularized in the 20th century, primarily in the United States. One of the first recorded usages is from the poem "Figs" by Edna St. Vincent Millay in 1920: "My candle burns at both ends; It will not last the night; But ah, my foes, and oh, my friends—It gives a lovely light!"

Example Sentence

"Between her full-time job and pursuing her master's degree at night, Sarah was burning the candle at both ends."

The idiom "burn the candle at both ends" paints an evocative image of depletion. Just as a candle lit at both ends will not last, a person pushing themselves relentlessly will eventually face exhaustion. The phrase is a poignant reminder of the importance of balance. While hard work and ambition are commendable, continuously overextending oneself without rest or recovery can lead to burnout. In a world that often glorifies busyness, the idiom serves as a cautionary tale about the price one might pay for neglecting self-care and well-being.

Work and Business

Climb the Corporate Ladder

To "climb the corporate ladder" means to advance or progress through the hierarchy of positions or ranks within a corporate or business environment. Typically, it involves moving from lower-level or entry positions to higher, more responsible roles, often accompanied by increased pay, prestige, and decision-making power.

Origin

1. Ladder as a Symbol: The ladder has long been a symbol of ascension, progress, and elevation, not only in English but in other languages and cultures too. In various religious and mythological contexts, ladders represent a connection between the earth and the heavens, or the journey of the soul.

2. Industrial and Corporate Evolution: The phrase likely has its roots in the 19th and early 20th centuries during the time of rapid industrialization and the emergence of modern corporations. As businesses grew in size and complexity, structured hierarchies became more pronounced, leading to distinct career paths where one could start at the bottom and work their way up.

3. 20th Century Usage: The exact phrase, "climb the corporate ladder," gained traction in the 20th century, particularly in post-WWII America, as the corporate world expanded and offered significant opportunities for upward mobility to employees dedicated to their careers.

Example Sentence

"Jenna started as an intern, but she quickly showed her skills and determination, allowing her to climb the corporate ladder to her current position as a senior manager."

The idiom "climb the corporate ladder" captures the ambition, drive, and dedication associated with pursuing career advancement in the corporate world. It evokes an image of a structured path, where each rung represents a new position or level of responsibility, and climbing it requires effort, persistence, and sometimes strategy. However, this phrase is not without its critiques. Some see the corporate ladder as rigid and limiting, suggesting that not all career trajectories fit this linear path. Moreover, the competitive nature of climbing this proverbial ladder can sometimes overshadow the importance of job satisfaction, work-life balance, and other non-hierarchical measures of career success. Nevertheless, the idiom remains a powerful representation of ambition and upward mobility in the business world.

Burning the Midnight Oil

To "burn the midnight oil" means to work late into the night or early morning hours. It is often used to describe the act of studying or working hard and diligently, especially when one stays up well past their usual bedtime.

Origin

1. Historical Context: Before the widespread availability of electric lighting, people relied on oil lamps for illumination after dark. If someone were working late into the night, they would literally be burning oil to provide light. The reference to "midnight" emphasizes the lateness of the hour and thus the extra effort or dedication being displayed.

2. 16th Century References: The concept of working late by lamplight can be traced back to at least the 16th century. However, the exact phrase "burning the midnight oil" started to appear in English literature and writings more prominently in the 19th century.

3. Symbolism: The act of using an oil lamp during the quiet, solitary hours of midnight became symbolic of dedication, hard work, and sometimes contemplation. The burning lamp amidst the surrounding darkness also evokes imagery of persistence and perseverance against challenges or the pressure of time.

Example Sentence

"Preparing for her final exams, Maria was burning the midnight oil for several nights in a row."

The idiom "burning the midnight oil" paints a vivid picture of dedication and commitment. There's an inherent romanticism in the image of a lone individual, illuminated only by the glow of an oil lamp, immersed in their work or studies as the world sleeps. It underscores the sacrifices one might make in pursuit of a goal, be it academic excellence, a work project, or any endeavor that demands time and concentration. As with many idioms, its origins rooted in historical realities give it a rich depth, even as its modern usage has evolved to encapsulate any scenario of working or studying late, irrespective of actual lamps or oil.

Business as Usual

"Business as usual" refers to the continuation of regular operations and activities, despite external disruptions or unusual circumstances. Essentially, it means that things are proceeding as they normally would, even if there has been some event that might have interrupted them.

Origin

1. War Origins: The term is believed to have gained widespread prominence during the First World War. There's a popularly cited instance from December 1914 when, despite the onset of war, the British government and monarchy wanted to convey a sense of resilience and continuity. King George V is said to have used the phrase to communicate that, despite the war, the monarchy and the British institutions were still functioning as they always had.

2. Commercial Usage: The phrase was also used in commerce and trade during the same period. Shopkeepers and businesses would put up "business as usual" signs after air raids or bombings, indicating that they were open and functioning despite the damages. It was both a sign of resilience and a practical message to customers.

3. Evolution Over Time: Over the years, the phrase has been adopted in numerous contexts beyond war and commerce. It's now used in various situations to convey a sense of normalcy and continuity, regardless of disruptions or changes.

Example Sentence

"Despite the CEO's sudden resignation, it was business as usual at the company, with everyone continuing their work without missing a beat."

The idiom "business as usual" carries with it a sense of resilience, steadfastness, and determination. Its historical origins rooted in wartime and commerce convey the spirit of pushing forward despite adversity. The phrase has now become universal, extending beyond just business scenarios. Whether it's in the context of personal challenges or global events, "business as usual" encapsulates the human drive to maintain stability and continuity even in the face of unexpected disruptions. It also sometimes carries a critique, especially when used in scenarios where change might be necessary; "business as usual" can be perceived as an unwillingness to adapt or innovate. Regardless, the phrase remains a powerful testament to perseverance.

Cut Corners

To "cut corners" means to take shortcuts or to find a cheaper, easier, or faster way to do something, often at the expense of quality, safety, or integrity. It suggests a deviation from the proper or traditional way of doing things, typically to save time or money.

Origin

1. Literal Interpretation: The term can be understood quite literally. Imagine a person walking along a sidewalk, and instead of following the entire path, they take a diagonal shortcut across a grassy corner to save time. This act of cutting across rather than walking the full perimeter is more efficient but might be seen as improper or even damaging (to the grass, in this instance).

2. Carpentry & Building: Another possible origin comes from carpentry and building. Instead of carefully measuring and crafting each piece, a carpenter might "cut corners" to save on materials or to work faster, which might affect the final quality or stability of the structure.

3. Industrial Age: As industries grew and mass production became more prevalent, there were increasing pressures to produce more in less time and at a reduced cost. "Cutting corners" would have been a way for factories and businesses to increase profit margins by skimping on quality or ignoring certain standards.

Example Sentence

"To finish the project by the deadline, they decided to cut corners, but this led to several issues down the line."

The idiom "cut corners" encapsulates the tension between efficiency and integrity. On one hand, finding quicker and more efficient methods can be seen as innovative and smart. On the other hand, when this results in compromised quality, safety, or ethics, "cutting corners" is viewed negatively. The phrase is often used as a cautionary note, suggesting that while shortcuts might provide immediate gains, they could lead to long-term problems or deficiencies. In contemporary times, especially in a world that often emphasizes speed and cost-effectiveness, "cut corners" serves as a reminder of the importance of diligence, quality, and upholding standards.

Get the Ball Rolling

To "get the ball rolling" means to start a process or to set something into motion. It's often used to refer to initiating an activity or project, especially one that requires continued effort or momentum.

Origin

1. Sports Imagery: The idiom can be visualized quite literally from various sports or games where a ball is set into motion, such as bowling, croquet, or billiards. In these games, once the ball starts rolling, the game progresses.

2. Historical Context: The earliest documented use of a similar phrase "set the ball rolling" dates back to the 18th century. In this context, its likely referenced activities or events where an actual ball was put into motion, signifying the start or commencement of the event.

3. Expansion and Popularization: Over time, the phrase was abstracted from its sports or game origin and began to be applied to various scenarios, from initiating conversations to commencing major projects. The idiom evolved, and both "set the ball rolling" and "get the ball rolling" have been used, with the latter becoming more prevalent in modern English.

Example Sentence

"We've been talking about this fundraiser for weeks; it's time to get the ball rolling and begin our planning in earnest."

The idiom "get the ball rolling" beautifully illustrates the idea of initiation and momentum. Much like in games where setting the ball in motion determines the course of play, in real-life projects or endeavors, starting off correctly and with enthusiasm often sets the tone for subsequent activities. This phrase is particularly handy when emphasizing the importance of a strong or efficient start. It conveys a sense of action and progress, suggesting that once things are set into motion, they will continue to move forward, potentially gathering speed and support as they go. It serves as a motivational call, urging individuals or groups to transition from contemplation or discussion into actual, tangible action.

Have a Lot on One's Plate

To "have a lot on one's plate" means to be very busy, overwhelmed, or to have many tasks, duties, or responsibilities to deal with or manage at a particular time.

Origin

1. Literal Interpretation: The imagery behind this idiom can be easily visualized from the dining table context. If you imagine a plate filled with an abundance of food, it's indicative of having a lot to consume or process. In a similar manner, when someone has many responsibilities or tasks, their metaphorical plate is full, suggesting they have a great deal to handle or "digest".

2. Historical Usage: While the exact origin is hard to pinpoint, the idiom is believed to have been in use since at least the late 19th to early 20th century. It is a testament to its relatability, given that the act of eating and the notion of a filled plate are universal experiences. Over time, the phrase transitioned from a literal context of food to symbolizing life's various responsibilities.

3. Cultural Context: It's interesting to note that while the expression is widely understood in English-speaking countries, the sentiment it conveys is universally felt. Different cultures might have their own unique ways of expressing this feeling of being overwhelmed with tasks or responsibilities.

Example Sentence

"With the upcoming merger and his daughter's wedding next month, Robert feels like he has a lot on his plate."

The phrase "have a lot on one's plate" resonates with many because it captures a universal sentiment of juggling multiple tasks or facing overwhelming situations. Drawing from the relatable imagery of a filled dining plate, it metaphorically illustrates the idea of capacity—just as a plate can only hold so much food, an individual has limits to how much they can handle at a given time. In today's fast-paced world, where multitasking is often the norm, this idiom serves as a succinct way to express the feeling of being stretched thin or being burdened with numerous obligations.

Jump Through Hoops

To "jump through hoops" means to go through many difficult or tedious obstacles, tasks, or challenges, often involving bureaucracy, in order to achieve a specific goal or objective.

Origin

1. Circus Origins: The phrase has strong ties to circus performances. In circuses, animals, particularly dogs, lions, or tigers, were trained to jump through hoops as a part of their acts. It was a testament to the trainer's skill and the animal's obedience. Sometimes, these hoops would even be set aflame, making the feat even more daring and impressive.

2. Metaphorical Application: As audiences watched these circus acts, they couldn't help but appreciate the effort, skill, and sometimes danger involved in such performances. The metaphorical jump from the literal circus act to describing the challenges and obstacles people face in daily life or bureaucratic situations wasn't a far one. Over time, the phrase began to symbolize not just the physical challenges of a circus act, but the metaphorical challenges of navigating complex, often frustrating, situations.

3. Expansion of Usage: The term became a way to express the effort required to navigate red tape, fulfill multiple, often seemingly unnecessary, requirements, or simply put in significant effort to achieve something.

Example Sentence

"Getting approval for the new park required us to jump through so many bureaucratic hoops, but it was worth it in the end."

"Jump through hoops" vividly conveys the idea of effort, tenacity, and sometimes the exasperation of navigating challenges, especially those that seem superfluous or overly complicated. Drawing from the rich visual imagery of the circus, it highlights the lengths to which one might go to achieve a goal, especially in the face of unnecessary or redundant obstacles. The idiom taps into a shared human experience of facing and overcoming challenges, making it a powerful expression in the English language.

Pull One's Weight

Meaning

To "pull one's weight" means to do one's fair share of the work or to contribute adequately to a group effort. It suggests that each person in a team or group has responsibilities, and everyone is expected to participate or contribute equally.

Origin

1. Nautical Origins: One of the early contexts where this phrase was used was in rowing. When a team of people are rowing a boat, it's crucial for each person to contribute equally. If one person isn't rowing as hard or as effectively as the others (i.e., not pulling their weight), it can throw off the boat's balance, rhythm, and speed.

2. Team Animals and Workload: Another origin point can be traced back to the use of animals, particularly horses, in tasks like farming or pulling carts. When two horses were yoked together, it was essential for both animals to pull equally. If one horse lagged behind or didn't pull as hard, the other horse would have to overcompensate, leading to inefficiency and potential harm.

3. Evolution Over Time: As industries evolved and team efforts became common in various fields, the phrase began to be applied more broadly. It transitioned from a literal physical context to a metaphorical one, representing the idea of each member of a group or team contributing their fair share to the collective effort.

Example Sentence

"In any group project, it's important for every member to pull their weight to ensure the task gets completed on time."

The idiom "pull one's weight" taps into a fundamental aspect of teamwork and cooperation. In any collaborative endeavor, the contributions of each individual matter. Just as in the literal scenarios of rowing a boat or yoking animals together, the metaphorical application of this phrase underscores the idea that shared efforts yield the best results. The idiom serves as a reminder of the responsibilities one has to their team or group and the negative consequences of shirking those responsibilities. It emphasizes the importance of collective effort and the value of each individual's contribution.

Throw in the Towel

Meaning

To "throw in the towel" means to admit defeat, to give up, or to acknowledge that continuing in a particular endeavor is futile or pointless.

Origin

1. Boxing Origins: The idiom derives from the world of boxing. When a boxer's cornerman, usually the trainer or manager, believed that the boxer was taking too much punishment in the ring or had no chance of winning, they would throw a towel into the ring as a signal to the referee to stop the fight. This act symbolized surrender or admission that their boxer could not continue.

2. Historical Context: The practice of using a towel as a sign of forfeit in boxing dates back to the early 20th century. Before towels became the standard, other items like sponges (which were used to clean and refresh fighters between rounds) were thrown into the ring to indicate a fighter's wish to concede.

3. Cultural Evolution: While the act started in boxing, the phrase soon began to be used metaphorically in other contexts. It became synonymous with giving up or admitting defeat in any situation, not just in the context of a physical fight. The phrase became ingrained in popular culture and was adopted in various languages as a way of expressing surrender or resignation in the face of insurmountable odds.

Example Sentence

"After years of trying to make the business work and facing continuous losses, Maria decided to throw in the towel and pursue a different career."

"Throw in the towel" captures the essence of human struggle, perseverance, and the eventual realization when a situation is untenable. Drawing from the vivid imagery of a pivotal moment in a boxing match, this idiom encapsulates the emotion of conceding in the face of adversity. Its widespread use across different contexts and cultures underscores a universal human experience: knowing when to continue fighting and when to accept defeat for the sake of one's well-being or larger goals.

Seal the Deal

To "seal the deal" means to finalize or confirm an agreement, arrangement, or transaction. It signifies the act of conclusively settling a matter or making a final decision. The phrase is commonly used in business contexts but can also be used in various other situations where an agreement or decision is reached.

Origin

1. Historical Transactions: Historically, formal transactions, particularly legal documents or important contracts, were sealed with wax. A person would melt wax onto the document and then press a seal (often a ring or a specially designed hand-held seal) into the wax, imprinting it with a unique design or crest. This act symbolically represented the authenticity, security, and finality of the document's contents.

2. The Weight of Seals: The use of seals carried significant weight. In many societies, a seal acted as a person's signature, a mark of their word and bond. Breaking or violating what was sealed was seen as a grave act, whether it was breaking a sealed letter meant for someone else or violating the terms of a sealed agreement.

3. Metaphorical Transition: Over time, as formal wax seals became less common, the term evolved and began to be used metaphorically. "Sealing the deal" retained its connotations of finality, authenticity, and commitment but began to refer to the broader act of confirming or finalizing an agreement, even if no physical seal was involved.

Example Sentence

"After months of negotiations, they finally managed to seal the deal with the international partners, ensuring the company's expansion into new markets."

The idiom "seal the deal" resonates with the gravitas of historical agreements and the solemnity with which they were treated. Drawing from the tangible and ceremonial act of sealing documents, it emphasizes the importance of commitment, trustworthiness, and finality in modern-day agreements and decisions. The phrase serves as a bridge between ancient practices and contemporary negotiations, reflecting the timeless nature of human agreements and the weight they carry in shaping individual and collective destinies.

Break Even

Meaning

To "break even" means to have one's costs equal one's gains or earnings. In other words, when a person or business breaks even, they haven't made a profit, but they also haven't incurred a loss. The income or returns are precisely sufficient to cover the expenses or costs.

Origin

1. Economic and Financial Roots: The term originates from the world of finance and business. When analyzing the financial performance of a business, particularly its profitability, "breaking even" is a key metric. It represents the point where total revenues match total costs or expenses, resulting in neither profit nor loss.

2. Break-even Point: The concept is further detailed in the "break-even point," a critical measure in accounting and finance. This point is calculated by dividing the total fixed costs by the difference between the unit selling price and the variable costs per unit. It tells a business how many units it must sell to cover its costs before it can start making a profit.

3. Evolution of the Term: While rooted in financial contexts, the term has evolved and is now used more broadly to describe situations outside of business where inputs and outputs, or efforts and rewards, balance out. It's employed in diverse contexts, from personal finance to sports, indicating a position of neither advantage nor disadvantage.

Example Sentence

"After factoring in the costs of materials, labor, and marketing, the company hopes to break even in the first year and then start making a profit in the second."

The idiom "break even" underscores the delicate balance many businesses and individuals navigate between success and setback, profit and loss. Rooted deeply in the world of economics, it serves as a touchstone for understanding financial health and planning for future sustainability. The broader adoption of this phrase in everyday language highlights its relatability and the universal understanding of the tightrope walk between gains and losses in various aspects of life.

In the Red

When one is "in the red," it indicates a financial loss or debt. In accounting and finance, if a company or individual's books are "in the red," it means they are operating at a deficit or are losing money. The term is often used to describe bank accounts, financial statements, or any situation where expenses exceed income.

Origin

1. Accounting Ledgers: Historically, accountants used ledgers to record financial transactions. When noting profits, they would often write in black ink, while deficits or losses were recorded in red ink. The use of different colors made it easier to quickly identify positive from negative figures.

2. Red for Warning: The color red has been universally associated with caution or danger. In financial contexts, red ink served as a clear visual warning of a problem or concern. This dual meaning reinforced the association between financial losses and the color red.

3. Modern Usage: As technology evolved and physical ledgers gave way to digital spreadsheets and systems, the concept of "in the red" persisted. Many digital interfaces, like spreadsheets or online banking platforms, still use red to highlight negative figures or overdrafts.

Example Sentence

"After a series of poor investments, the company found itself deep in the red and had to consider drastic measures to recover."

The phrase "in the red" connects the tangible world of ink and paper with the abstract realm of finance and economics. Its origin in the ledgers of accountants provides a vivid and straightforward visualization of a complex concept: financial loss. The term serves as a beacon, alerting businesses and individuals to situations that require attention or correction. By bridging the past with the present, "in the red" remains a testament to the timeless challenges and practices of financial management.

On the Back Burner

To put something "on the back burner" means to postpone or delay dealing with it, often because it's currently less urgent or important than other matters. It suggests that while something is not being actively addressed, it hasn't been forgotten and will be attended to later.

Origin

1. Kitchen Origins: The idiom is believed to have originated from the practice of cooking on a stove with multiple burners. When preparing multiple dishes, the burners at the front are typically used for items that need immediate or constant attention, while the burners at the back (the "back burners") are used for dishes that can simmer or be left unattended for a longer period.

2. Prioritizing Tasks: Just as a cook prioritizes which dishes need immediate attention on the front burners and which can simmer on the back burners, the phrase transitioned to a metaphorical context. It began to represent the idea of prioritizing tasks or issues based on their urgency or importance.

3. Evolution in Usage: Over time, the idiom shifted from the realm of cooking to general everyday language. It is now applied in diverse settings, from business to personal matters, to convey the idea of deferring or delaying something.

Example Sentence

"While the new website design is important, the company's current financial challenges have put that project on the back burner for now."

The idiom "on the back burner" beautifully encapsulates the constant juggling and prioritizing people and organizations engage in daily. Its roots in the tangible practice of cooking provide a relatable and intuitive understanding of how we decide what to address immediately and what can wait. This phrase serves as a reminder that while not everything can or should be tackled at once, things that are set aside aren't necessarily forgotten or deemed unimportant. They're merely awaiting their moment of primary focus.

Think Outside the Box

To "think outside the box" means to think creatively, unconventionally, or from a fresh perspective. It suggests the need to approach a problem or situation in a novel way rather than relying on traditional or established methods.

Origin

1. 9-Dot Puzzle: One commonly cited origin of the idiom traces back to a popular puzzle known as the nine-dot problem. In this puzzle, individuals are presented with nine dots arranged in a square and are tasked with connecting all the dots using just four straight lines without lifting the pen. The solution requires drawing lines that extend beyond the "box" formed by the dots, thus necessitating "thinking outside the box."

2. Corporate Lingo: By the late 20th century, the phrase had become a popular piece of corporate jargon. It was widely used in business settings to encourage employees and teams to innovate and come up with unconventional solutions to problems.

3. Wider Cultural Adoption: While the phrase's roots might lie in puzzles and business environments, its resonance with the idea of breaking free from constraints ensured that it found its way into broader cultural and societal lexicons.

Example Sentence

"To solve this challenging issue, we'll need to think outside the box and explore solutions we haven't considered before."

The idiom "think outside the box" champions the spirit of innovation and creativity. At its core, it's an exhortation to break free from self-imposed or societal limitations and to see beyond the obvious. It stands as a testament to the human capacity for ingenuity and our inherent desire to push boundaries and redefine what's possible. In an ever-evolving world, this phrase serves as both a challenge and a reminder of the power of unconventional thinking.

From the Ground Up

Meaning

To build or develop something "from the ground up" means to start from the very beginning, often from nothing, and to develop it fully and thoroughly. It implies starting from the most basic level and working one's way through all the stages until completion.

Origin

1. Architectural and Construction Roots: The phrase likely originates from the world of construction and architecture. When a building is constructed "from the ground up," it starts with laying the foundation on raw land and then building upwards until the structure is complete.

2. Comprehensive Development: This idea of starting with the foundational and elemental aspects and progressing systematically is inherent in the phrase. It underscores the meticulous and complete nature of the endeavor, be it the building of a physical structure or any other project.

3. Wider Application: Over time, the phrase transcended its architectural origins and began to be applied to a plethora of situations outside of construction, like developing a business, crafting a skill, or creating software.

Example Sentence

"She built her company from the ground up, starting as a sole entrepreneur in her garage and eventually expanding into a global enterprise."

The idiom "from the ground up" evokes a sense of thoroughness, dedication, and painstaking effort. It conveys the narrative of an entity built with care, where every foundational piece is vital to the stability and success of the whole. Whether it's used to describe the establishment of a new venture or the learning of a new skill, the phrase emphasizes the importance of understanding and mastering every level or stage. It serves as a tribute to hard work, perseverance, and the journey of creating something substantial and lasting from scratch.

Rise to the Occasion

Meaning

To "rise to the occasion" means to succeed in dealing with a challenging situation or to perform better than usual in response to an extraordinary event or circumstance. It signifies a person's ability to muster resources, skills, or qualities they might not exhibit in ordinary situations to meet a particular challenge.

Origin

1. Historical Context: The idiom traces its origins back to the 18th century. Its early uses were often in the context of public speaking or performances where an individual was expected to "rise" or stand up to address an audience. To "rise to the occasion" meant to meet or exceed the expectations of the moment.

2. Metaphorical Evolution: The act of "rising" has long been metaphorically associated with meeting challenges. The vertical movement implies overcoming gravity and ascending, both of which require effort. Over time, "rise to the occasion" came to be understood more broadly, implying not just standing up physically, but also elevating one's capabilities, spirit, or behavior to tackle a challenge effectively.

3. Cultural Depictions: Literature, movies, and historical accounts often celebrate individuals who have "risen to the occasion." These stories of heroism, bravery, or sheer resilience in the face of adversity have solidified the idiom's place in the cultural lexicon.

Example Sentence

"When the team captain got injured during the crucial match, the youngest player rose to the occasion, leading the team to victory with his outstanding performance."

The idiom "rise to the occasion" speaks to the human potential to surpass one's own limits, especially when confronted with significant challenges. It captures the essence of resilience, adaptability, and the innate drive many possess to overcome obstacles. In a world filled with unexpected events and hurdles, the phrase serves as a beacon of hope and a testament to the human spirit's capacity to meet challenges head-on.

Touch Base

To "touch base" means to briefly make contact with someone, typically to update or check in on a particular situation. It's often used in the context of ensuring that people are on the same page or to maintain communication over an ongoing issue or task.

Origin

1. Baseball Origins: This idiom finds its roots in the sport of baseball. In baseball, runners need to touch each of the four bases to score a run. "Touching base" ensures that the runner is following the rules and is safe from being tagged out.

2. Business Jargon Adoption: Given its easily relatable concept, the phrase was soon co-opted into business and general lingo. In the corporate world, where continuous communication is essential, "touching base" became a way of saying "let's quickly check in with each other."

3. Evolution Over Time: While initially used mostly in professional environments, the phrase has since permeated everyday language. It's now commonly employed in various contexts where two or more individuals need to briefly connect or catch up on a topic.

Example Sentence

"I haven't heard from the client since our last meeting. I'll touch base with them tomorrow to see if they have any feedback on the proposal."

The idiom "touch base" encapsulates the essence of brief yet essential communication. Especially in a fast-paced world, where people are juggling multiple responsibilities, "touching base" signifies the importance of keeping communication lines open, ensuring alignment, and maintaining relationships. Whether in a professional setting or personal life, the phrase highlights the significance of brief check-ins to ensure clarity and mutual understanding.

Up the Ante

To "up the ante" means to increase the stakes or the risk in a situation, typically to pressure an opponent or to achieve a greater reward. In broader contexts, it refers to raising the standards, expectations, or investments in a particular scenario.

Origin

1. Poker Origins: The term "ante" comes from the world of poker, a card game where players bet money into a central pot. The "ante" is the initial bet that each player must make to participate in a hand. When someone chooses to "up the ante," they are increasing the initial bet, thus raising the potential winnings but also taking on a higher risk.

2. Wider Usage Beyond Card Games: As poker became popular and widely played, some of its terminologies seeped into everyday language. "Up the ante" became an idiom that went beyond the card table, capturing the essence of increasing stakes or making a situation more challenging.

3. Modern Application: Today, the phrase is used in a variety of situations, from business negotiations to personal challenges, where the intensity or stakes of the situation are being elevated.

Example Sentence

"As the deadline approached, the client upped the ante by adding new requirements, increasing the pressure on the development team."

The idiom "up the ante" captures the dynamics of challenge and risk. It speaks to the human tendency to not remain content with the status quo, pushing boundaries, and taking greater risks in pursuit of bigger rewards. The phrase also touches on strategy, as increasing the stakes can be a calculated move to test and influence the behavior of opponents or collaborators. Whether one is aiming for a higher return on investment, setting more ambitious goals, or negotiating more aggressively, "upping the ante" underscores the importance of risk-taking and strategy in achieving success.

Go Down the Drain

To "go down the drain" means to become wasted or lost, especially after an investment of time, effort, or resources. It can refer to opportunities, finances, or any kind of investment that has been rendered useless or has not resulted in the expected outcome.

Origin

1. Literal Interpretation: The phrase has its roots in the literal action of water (or any liquid) going down a drain, leaving nothing behind. When something goes down a drain, it disappears and often cannot be retrieved.

2. Societal Changes and Plumbing: With the popularization of indoor plumbing in the 19th and 20th centuries, the visual of things disappearing down drains became a commonplace sight in households. Over time, this observation started being used metaphorically to describe wasted efforts or resources.

3. Economic Context: The phrase gained traction during economic downturns, where investments or efforts could become futile due to external market conditions. As individuals and businesses experienced losses, the visual metaphor of resources or opportunities "going down the drain" became particularly poignant.

Example Sentence

"After the company's major project failed, all the months of hard work seemed to go down the drain."

The idiom "go down the drain" vividly captures the despair and disappointment of seeing one's efforts or investments come to naught. The visual of something irretrievably disappearing down a drain serves as a stark metaphor for lost opportunities, wasted resources, or unfruitful endeavors. In various spheres of life, from personal aspirations to business projects, the phrase is a reminder of the unpredictability of outcomes and the potential risks inherent in any venture. Whether one is recounting financial losses or lamenting missed opportunities, "going down the drain" encapsulates the sense of something valuable being lost forever.

A Dime a Dozen

Meaning

The idiom "a dime a dozen" refers to something that is very common, easily obtainable, or lacking in uniqueness or special value. When something is described as "a dime a dozen," it suggests that it's not particularly special or rare.

Origin

1. Historical Context: The phrase dates back to the 19th and early 20th centuries in the United States. Dimes, being a small denomination of currency, were used to buy various cheap items. Additionally, during certain periods, inflation and other economic factors made certain goods very affordable.

2. Marketing and Mass Production: As methods of mass production took hold in the early 20th century, many products became widely available at low costs. Advertisements during this era might literally offer items at "a dime a dozen" to emphasize their affordability. Over time, the phrase started to take on a more figurative meaning, indicating not just cost but also commonality.

3. Shift in Value Perception: As goods that were "a dime a dozen" were cheap and plentiful; they were often perceived as being of lesser quality or value. This perception then expanded beyond just products to refer to ideas, opportunities, or even people, suggesting that they were commonplace and not of unique value.

Example Sentence

"With so many singers trying to make it in the music industry, talented vocalists are a dime a dozen, but true stage presence is rare."

The idiom "a dime a dozen" encapsulates the idea that not everything that is easily available or common holds significant value. It speaks to the human tendency to value rarity and uniqueness. In a world saturated with information, products, and talents, the phrase serves as a reminder that true worth often lies not in sheer numbers but in distinctiveness and quality. Whether one is assessing opportunities, evaluating goods, or considering skills, "a dime a dozen" challenges us to look beyond the commonplace and seek out the truly exceptional.

Conflict and Resolution

Bury the Hatchet

Meaning

The idiom "bury the hatchet" means to make peace or to settle one's differences with someone. When two parties "bury the hatchet," they are agreeing to put aside their grievances and move forward in a positive or neutral manner.

Origin

1. Historical Context: The phrase originates from a Native American custom, particularly among tribes of the northeastern United States. When tribes or individuals within tribes decided to make peace after conflicts or disputes, they would hold a ceremony where a hatchet or tomahawk (a type of small axe) was buried into the ground. This symbolized the cessation of hostilities and the intention to start afresh without violence.

2. Cultural Significance: The act of burying a weapon in the ground was a powerful symbolic gesture. By doing so, the tribes or individuals were not only signaling their commitment to peace but were also making a physical action to render a weapon of war unusable, showcasing their genuine intent.

3. Adoption into English Language: Over time, English settlers and Native American tribes had various interactions, some peaceful and others hostile. The settlers adopted and adapted many native phrases and practices, including this one. The idiom "bury the hatchet" began to be used in English to denote the act of reconciliation.

Example Sentence

"After years of rivalry, the two companies decided to bury the hatchet and collaborate on a joint venture."

The idiom "bury the hatchet" speaks to the universal human desire for peace and reconciliation. It underscores the importance of letting go of past grievances to forge a better future. The transition of this phrase from a literal act of peace among tribes to a widely used figurative expression in the English language is a testament to the deep-seated human need to resolve conflicts and move forward in harmony.

At Loggerheads

The idiom "at loggerheads" means to be in strong disagreement or dispute with someone. When two parties are "at loggerheads," they are deeply entrenched in an argument or conflict and find it hard to come to a resolution.

Origin

1. Historical Context: The exact origin of the phrase is debated, but one of the more accepted theories is that it derives from the 17th-century term "loggerhead," which was a type of iron instrument with a long handle. This tool was heated and used for melting pitch. In some contexts, loggerheads were also used in shipboard fights, where opposing parties would strike each other with these implements.

2. Figurative Transition: Over time, "loggerheads" came to symbolize conflict or clashing, possibly due to the violent nature of the shipboard fights or because of the image of two heated loggerheads being brought into contact, producing sparks. This transitioned into the phrase "at loggerheads" to represent two parties butting heads or in disagreement.

3. Linguistic Evolution: The term "loggerhead" itself is older, with references to it being used to mean a "stupid person" or "blockhead" in the 16th century. However, its connection to the idiom and the notion of conflict likely comes from its association with the tool and the aforementioned confrontations.

Example Sentence

"The two neighboring countries have been at loggerheads over the border dispute for decades."

The idiom "at loggerheads" captures the intensity and stubbornness often present in prolonged disputes. It illustrates how disagreements can escalate to the point where resolution seems distant, echoing the imagery of two forces colliding without yielding. The evolution and continued usage of the phrase serve as a linguistic testament to the challenges of resolving deeply rooted conflicts.

Beat Around the Bush

Meaning

The idiom "beat around the bush" refers to avoiding a direct or clear response, or delaying getting to the point of a matter. When someone is said to be "beating around the bush," they are avoiding the main topic, often out of hesitation, reluctance, or diplomacy.

Origin

1. Historical Context: This expression has its roots in medieval hunting techniques. When hunting birds, beaters would be employed to strike the bushes, causing birds to take flight and making them easier targets for hunters. Instead of directly approaching the prey (the birds), they would beat the areas around it, which is where the notion of indirectness or avoidance in the idiom comes from.

2. Figurative Adoption: Over time, the action of beating around the bush instead of directly targeting the prey became symbolic of approaching a subject in a roundabout manner. The phrase began to be used metaphorically in the English language by the 16th century to describe the act of avoiding a main issue or not speaking directly about a topic.

3. Modern Usage: The idiom's continued relevance and usage in modern English show the human tendency to sometimes approach sensitive or difficult topics with caution, hesitance, or tact, rather than addressing them head-on.

Example Sentence

"Instead of beating around the bush, please tell me exactly what you think about my proposal."

The idiom "beat around the bush" highlights a universal human behavior of sometimes avoiding directness, especially when faced with uncomfortable, sensitive, or challenging topics. Whether used in a criticism or an understanding manner, the phrase acts as a mirror to human communication intricacies, reflecting the dance between diplomacy and directness.

Seeing Eye to Eye

Meaning

The idiom "seeing eye to eye" refers to two or more individuals agreeing on a matter or having the same opinion about a particular subject. When people "see eye to eye," they understand and concur with each other without any significant disagreement.

Origin

1. Biblical Roots: The phrase has origins in the Bible. In the Book of Isaiah (Isaiah 52:8), the term is used: "Thy watchmen shall lift up the voice; with the voice together shall they sing: for they shall see eye to eye, when the Lord shall bring again Zion." In this context, it signifies a shared vision or understanding.

2. Physical Connotation: On a more literal level, when two individuals stand face-to-face and look directly into each other's eyes, they are "seeing eye to eye." This physical closeness can metaphorically imply a close agreement or understanding between the parties involved.

3. Evolution over Time: Over time, the phrase transitioned from its biblical roots and began to be used more broadly in English literature and everyday speech to indicate agreement or shared perspective.

Example Sentence

"After hours of debate, the committee members finally saw eye to eye on the budget proposal."

The idiom "seeing eye to eye" captures the essence of harmony, understanding, and mutual agreement. In a world where differing opinions and viewpoints abound, the ability to "see eye to eye" with someone is often seen as a commendable and sometimes rare achievement. The phrase underscores the importance of finding common ground and understanding in both personal and professional relationships. It reminds us that while disagreements are natural, arriving at mutual understanding is both possible and beneficial.

Cross Swords

Meaning

The idiom "cross swords" means to engage in an argument, dispute, or conflict with someone. When individuals "cross swords," they are clashing or opposing each other on a particular issue or set of issues.

Origin

1. Historical Dueling: The phrase has direct ties to the medieval and Renaissance practice of dueling. Dueling was a formalized combat between two individuals, usually with weapons like swords, to resolve a dispute or defend one's honor. When opponents met in a duel, the first act was often to cross their swords, indicating the commencement of the battle.

2. Symbolism of Swords: Swords have long been symbols of power, honor, and combat. The act of crossing swords not only signified the beginning of a duel but also represented opposing forces meeting head-on.

3. Figurative Transition: As the practice of dueling waned and became more metaphorical in nature, the idiom began to represent verbal arguments or disagreements rather than physical battles. The imagery of two swords clashing served as a vivid representation of two parties in opposition.

Example Sentence

"Although they were close friends, they would often cross swords over their differing political views."

The idiom "cross swords" encapsulates the age-old human tendency to engage in conflicts, debates, and disagreements. By drawing on the imagery of dueling, it emphasizes the intensity and directness of confrontations. Whether used to describe a friendly debate or a more heated disagreement, the phrase serves as a reminder of the importance of understanding, compromise, and finding common ground even in the face of opposition.

Kiss and Make Up

The idiom "kiss and make up" refers to the act of reconciling or settling one's differences after a disagreement or quarrel. When people "kiss and make up," they are putting their past disputes behind them and restoring friendly or amiable relations.

Origin

1. Literal and Figurative Affection: The act of kissing is a universal gesture of affection and intimacy. Historically, a kiss could serve multiple purposes, from a sign of love and respect to a ritualized greeting. In many cultures, making up after a disagreement often involved some gesture of physical affection or closeness, hence the link between the act of kissing and reconciliation.

2. Emphasis on Restoration: The phrase emphasizes not just the act of resolving disagreements, but also the subsequent restoration of friendly relations. Making up denotes the process of coming to a resolution, and the kiss symbolizes the renewed warmth and closeness between the parties.

3. Popular Usage: The idiom gained traction in popular culture, especially in romantic contexts where couples would often have disagreements, only to later reconcile their differences with affection. Its catchy, rhyming nature also made it memorable and easily adopted into everyday language.

Example Sentence

"After a heated argument about their holiday plans, the couple decided to kiss and make up, realizing that spending time together was more important than the destination."

The idiom "kiss and make up" underscores the importance of reconciliation and the human capacity for forgiveness. It highlights the transient nature of most disagreements when viewed against the backdrop of enduring relationships and the significance of restoring bonds of affection and understanding. Whether used in a romantic context or more broadly, the phrase serves as a hopeful reminder that rifts can be healed and relationships mended.

Stir the Pot

The idiom "stir the pot" refers to the act of causing unrest or provoking trouble, often by instigating disagreements or reviving controversial issues. When someone is said to be "stirring the pot," they are intentionally trying to create drama or tension within a group or situation.

Origin

1. Cooking Analogy: The literal act of stirring a pot is a common step in cooking. If a pot's contents are not stirred, ingredients may settle at the bottom and burn, or flavors might not mix well. In this context, stirring ensures an even distribution and prevents undesirable outcomes. However, when taken figuratively, this constant agitation can lead to unrest or heightened tensions, much like continuously stirring up topics or issues can lead to disputes or disagreements.

2. Figurative Transition: Over time, the phrase began to be used metaphorically to describe someone who keeps issues, especially contentious ones, in constant motion or brings up subjects that are likely to cause disagreement or controversy.

3. Modern Usage: In today's context, the idiom often has a negative connotation, as it usually refers to individuals who take pleasure in causing discord or those who seek to benefit from creating divisions among others.

Example Sentence

"Every time the team seemed to come to an agreement, Jake would bring up a new point of contention, always trying to stir the pot."

The idiom "stir the pot" offers a glimpse into human dynamics, particularly in group settings where unity and harmony can sometimes be disrupted by intentional provocations. Drawing from a simple cooking analogy, the phrase emphasizes the potential negative outcomes of unnecessary agitation. It serves as a reminder of the importance of fostering understanding and collaboration rather than continuously reviving sources of discord.

Clear the Air

The idiom "clear the air" refers to the act of resolving misunderstandings, dissipating tensions, or addressing issues that have caused confusion or conflict. When individuals "clear the air," they aim to restore harmony and understanding, typically through open communication.

Origin

1. Natural Phenomenon: The literal idea behind "clearing the air" derives from the natural occurrence of the atmosphere clearing up after a storm or a period of fog. Just as the weather can transition from being stormy or foggy to clear and calm, so can emotions and misunderstandings be resolved and clarified.

2. Figurative Transition: The metaphorical use of the phrase to mean resolving issues or dispelling doubts is a testament to the human practice of associating atmospheric or environmental changes with emotional or interpersonal shifts. Just as the environment can feel oppressive during a storm and refreshing afterward, discussions or confrontations that clear misunderstandings can provide relief and clarity.

3. Modern Usage: In contemporary language, the idiom is commonly used in both personal and professional settings. It encourages open dialogue as a means to address and alleviate underlying tensions or misapprehensions.

Example Sentence

"After the disagreement in the morning meeting, the team gathered in the afternoon to clear the air and ensure everyone was on the same page."

The idiom "clear the air" emphasizes the importance of open communication and confronting issues head-on to maintain harmonious relationships. It suggests that much like the natural world benefits from the cleansing nature of a storm, human interactions can similarly benefit from addressing and resolving conflicts. The phrase serves as an encouraging reminder that conflicts or misunderstandings, once addressed, often lead to clearer and more positive dynamics.

Add Fuel to the Fire

The idiom "add fuel to the fire" describes the act of making a situation or conflict worse, often by adding more information, provocation, or action that exacerbates the problem. When someone "adds fuel to the fire," they are intensifying or aggravating an already problematic or contentious situation.

Origin

1. Literal Interpretation: At its core, this idiom draws from the basic understanding of fire behavior. If you add fuel to an existing fire, it will burn hotter and more fiercely. In the same vein, adding more provocative elements to an argument or dispute will often inflame the situation further.

2. Ancient Usage: Variants of this idiom have existed for centuries. The concept of exacerbating an already difficult situation is universal, so many languages and cultures have expressions conveying this idea, often using the imagery of fire, which is universally recognized as something that can grow out of control if fed.

3. Modern Context: In today's usage, the idiom is often applied to situations where someone's actions or words unnecessarily worsen a situation, especially if they were aware of the potential for escalation and proceeded anyway.

Example Sentence

"Sarah was already upset about the mistake, but when John criticized her in front of the team, it just added fuel to the fire."

The idiom "add fuel to the fire" serves as a cautionary phrase, reminding us of the potential consequences of our actions and words, especially in sensitive or volatile situations. It underscores the importance of being aware and considerate, emphasizing the potential dangers of escalating conflicts. The vivid imagery of a fire growing out of control paints a clear picture of how quickly situations can deteriorate when provoked or mishandled.

Meet Halfway

Meaning

The idiom "meet halfway" refers to the act of compromising or making concessions in order to come to an agreement with someone. When two parties "meet halfway," they both give up some of their demands or desires to find a middle ground that is acceptable to both.

Origin

1. Literal Interpretation: The phrase likely stems from the tangible idea of two people traveling towards each other and meeting at a central point, equidistant from their starting locations. This physical act of meeting in the middle symbolizes equal effort and compromise.

2. Symbolism of Compromise: The midpoint represents a place of balance and equity. Just as two individuals can meet at a central location by traversing equal distances, they can also find common ground in negotiations or disputes by making equivalent concessions.

3. Historical and Cultural Context: The concept of compromise and negotiation has been vital throughout history in diplomacy, trade, and personal relationships. The imagery of "meeting halfway" effectively encapsulates this spirit of give and take.

Example Sentence

"While Anna wanted to vacation in the mountains and Rob preferred the beach, they decided to meet halfway and chose a lakeside retreat."

The idiom "meet halfway" emphasizes the importance of collaboration, compromise, and mutual respect. It serves as a reminder that in many conflicts or disagreements, both parties often have valid perspectives. By meeting halfway, they acknowledge the value in each other's positions and demonstrate a willingness to work together towards a solution. In a world of diverse opinions and desires, the phrase champions the idea that harmonious outcomes often arise from shared efforts and mutual concessions.

On the Warpath

The idiom "on the warpath" describes someone who is extremely angry and is preparing to confront or challenge someone else, often in an aggressive manner. When a person is said to be "on the warpath," it implies that they are actively seeking out conflict or are in a combative mood.

Origin

1. Native American Context: The phrase has its roots in the descriptions of Native American tribes preparing for conflict or war. When tribes were gearing up for a confrontation, they were said to be on the "warpath," a term used by European settlers in North America. It was a literal path or route that warriors would take when heading into battle.

2. Cultural Misappropriation: Over time, the term began to be used more broadly in American English to describe anyone who appeared to be looking for a confrontation, not just in the context of Native American tribes. However, it's essential to recognize that such idiomatic uses can oversimplify and stereotype the rich and diverse cultures of Native American tribes.

3. Modern Usage: In today's context, "on the warpath" is usually used figuratively to indicate someone's intense anger or readiness for a confrontation, often over something they perceive as an injustice or grievance. While the phrase is still in use, it's essential to approach it with cultural sensitivity due to its origins.

Example Sentence

"After finding out that the project had been mishandled, the boss was on the warpath, demanding answers from everyone involved."

The idiom "on the warpath" captures the intensity and focus that individuals can exhibit when they are deeply aggrieved or angered. It serves as a vivid representation of the single-mindedness that can accompany such emotions. However, given its cultural origins, it's a reminder of the importance of using language thoughtfully and respectfully, acknowledging the historical and cultural contexts from which idioms arise.

Build Bridges

Meaning

The idiom "build bridges" refers to the act of fostering better understanding, relationships, or communication between people or groups, especially if there has been a previous conflict or misunderstanding. When someone tries to "build bridges," they are making efforts to reconnect, reconcile, or establish positive connections.

Origin

1. Literal Foundation: The literal concept of building a bridge is a powerful symbol of connection. Bridges are structures designed to span obstacles such as rivers or chasms, allowing individuals to cross from one side to another. This tangible act of linking two previously disconnected or distant areas serves as an apt metaphor for interpersonal or intergroup connections.

2. Symbolism of Connection: Just as a physical bridge provides a pathway for people to come together, the metaphorical act of building bridges implies the creation of pathways for understanding, collaboration, and reconciliation.

3. Historical and Social Context: Throughout history, the act of bridge-building has been recognized for its importance in trade, transportation, and communication. Similarly, in social and political contexts, individuals and groups that have played roles in mediating conflicts, fostering dialogues, or establishing connections have been revered for their bridge-building abilities.

Example Sentence

"Despite their differences, the two community leaders worked together to build bridges, ensuring that everyone felt heard and represented."

The idiom "build bridges" underscores the value of connection, understanding, and diplomacy in human interactions. It serves as a reminder that despite disagreements or differences, there is often a middle ground or a path to mutual respect. In a world where divisions can sometimes seem insurmountable, the phrase champions the idea that deliberate efforts towards reconciliation and unity can forge meaningful and lasting bonds.

Burn One's Bridges

The idiom "burn one's bridges" refers to the act of doing something that makes it impossible to return to an earlier state or condition, often by permanently damaging a relationship, situation, or opportunity. When someone "burns their bridges," they take actions that hinder their chances of going back or making amends.

Origin

1. Military Tactics: Historically, the act of physically burning bridges was a strategic move in warfare. Armies would burn bridges behind them to prevent an advancing enemy from following or to stop themselves from retreating, thereby committing wholly to their forward path.

2. Symbolism of Irreversible Actions: Burning a bridge, a critical connection between two places, serves as a powerful metaphor for irreversible decisions or actions that sever ties or end opportunities.

3. Expansion to Social Context: Over time, the phrase transitioned from its military origins to more social and personal contexts, referring to actions that might damage personal or professional relationships, often irrevocably.

Example Sentence

"By publicly criticizing his former employer, Jake knew he was burning his bridges, making it unlikely they'd ever hire him back."

The idiom "burn one's bridges" emphasizes the gravity of certain decisions and the potential long-term implications of our actions. It serves as a cautionary tale about the permanence of some choices and the importance of foresight and deliberation. While the phrase paints a vivid picture of definitive action, it also reminds us of the value of maintaining connections and considering the broader implications of our decisions.

Let Bygones Be Bygones

Meaning

The idiom "let bygones be bygones" conveys the idea of forgiving past offenses or forgetting old conflicts and moving on without holding grudges. When someone suggests to "let bygones be bygones," they are recommending a fresh start and an end to lingering resentments.

Origin

1. Word Origin The term "bygone" originates from the Middle English term "bygon," which means "that which has gone by" or simply "past." Thus, "bygones" refers to past events or situations.

2. Historical Usage: The phrase itself has been in use since at least the 16th century, and its sentiment—that of forgiveness and looking forward—has long-standing roots in many cultures and religious teachings.

3. Cultural Relevance: Over the years, the phrase has been reiterated in literature, speeches, and daily life, emphasizing the importance of letting go of past animosities and embracing reconciliation. The idea behind the idiom resonates universally, as holding onto past grudges is often viewed as detrimental to personal growth and communal harmony.

Example Sentence

"After years of disagreement over their family business, the two brothers decided to let bygones be bygones and start anew with mutual respect."

The idiom "let bygones be bygones" captures the essence of forgiveness and the value of moving forward without being weighed down by past grievances. It serves as a reminder of the fleeting nature of time and the significance of present relationships and opportunities. In promoting reconciliation, the phrase emphasizes the importance of harmony, understanding, and growth in human interactions, suggesting that, at times, the best way forward is to release old resentments and embrace the potential of the present.

Lock Horns

Meaning

The idiom "lock horns" refers to engaging in a conflict, argument, or confrontation with someone else. When two parties "lock horns," they are in strong disagreement and are clashing over their differences.

Origin

1. Natural Observation: The origin of the phrase comes from the behavior of certain animals, notably deer or rams, that fight by locking their horns together in a display of strength and dominance. This act of two animals pushing against each other with locked horns serves as a metaphor for human confrontations and disputes.

2. Symbolism of Combat: The imagery of two animals locked in combat is powerful and vivid. Just as these animals might engage in fierce battles over territory or mating rights, humans too can become entangled in intense arguments or confrontations over differences in opinion, values, or interests.

3. Historical Usage: Over time, the phrase transitioned from its direct observational origins to a figurative usage in human social interactions, representing any form of disagreement or confrontation, not necessarily physical.

Example Sentence

"Every time the topic of politics comes up, Jane and Kyle lock horns, as their views are completely opposite."

The idiom "lock horns" evokes the intensity and passion with which individuals can defend their beliefs or positions. It serves as a vivid representation of confrontations, be they friendly debates or serious disagreements. The phrase reminds us of the inherent nature of conflict in both the animal kingdom and human interactions. While locking horns can be a way to assert one's stance, it also underlines the importance of understanding, compromise, and finding common ground to resolve disagreements.

Mend Fences

Meaning

The idiom "mend fences" refers to the act of repairing a relationship or trying to reconcile after disagreements or conflicts. When someone seeks to "mend fences," they are making efforts to restore trust, understanding, or friendship that may have been damaged or strained.

Origin

1. Literal Association: The phrase stems from the tangible action of repairing a broken fence. Fences are built to establish boundaries, offer protection, or contain livestock. A broken or damaged fence fails to serve its purpose. Similarly, in human relationships, misunderstandings or conflicts can "break" the protective barriers of trust and respect. Thus, mending a physical fence can serve as a metaphor for repairing the damage done to a relationship.

2. Symbolism of Restoration: Just as a mended fence re-establishes boundaries and provides protection, efforts to mend fences in interpersonal relations aim to restore boundaries of trust, respect, and mutual understanding that have been breached.

3. Historical Usage: The idiom has been in use since at least the 19th century and captures a universally recognized sentiment about the importance of reconciliation and the proactive efforts it often requires.

Example Sentence

"After their heated argument, Maria took the initiative to mend fences with her sister by apologizing and expressing her desire to move past their differences."

The idiom "mend fences" emphasizes the value of reconciliation and the active role individuals can take in healing rifts or misunderstandings. It serves as a reminder that relationships, like physical structures, require maintenance and care. When strained or damaged, proactive efforts can restore their integrity. The phrase champions the idea of taking responsibility for one's actions and highlights the restorative power of understanding, communication, and forgiveness in human relationships.

Wipe the Slate Clean

Meaning

The idiom "wipe the slate clean" refers to starting anew, forgetting past mistakes or transgressions, and giving someone or something a fresh start without any preconceived judgments or prejudices. When you "wipe the slate clean," you are essentially offering or getting a chance to begin again without the burden of past mistakes or misunderstandings.

Origin

1. Chalk and Slate: Historically, slates and chalk were commonly used in schools for writing before the widespread use of paper. When a student or teacher wanted to start a new lesson or task, they would wipe away the old writing, providing a fresh, clean surface to begin anew. This physical act of cleaning the slate to start again became synonymous with the idea of fresh beginnings or second chances.

2. Symbolism of Renewal: The action of wiping away past marks and errors provides a strong visual representation of forgiveness, letting go, and embarking on a new path. Over time, this simple act of erasing old notes became a metaphor for fresh starts in broader contexts, including relationships, endeavors, and personal challenges.

3. Historical Usage: The phrase has been in use since the 19th century and has since been ingrained in various cultures to symbolize the idea of new beginnings and the opportunity to move past old mistakes.

Example Sentence

"After their disagreement, both parties agreed to wipe the slate clean and work together harmoniously."

The idiom "wipe the slate clean" encapsulates the human desire for redemption, second chances, and the ability to move past errors. It emphasizes the value of looking forward rather than being anchored by past mistakes. By evoking the straightforward act of erasing past notes, the phrase illustrates the powerful idea that, at any moment, individuals and groups have the capacity to redefine their path, let go of past burdens, and embrace new opportunities.

Smoke the Peace Pipe

Meaning

The idiom "smoke the peace pipe" means to make peace, reconcile, or resolve differences with someone. When people "smoke the peace pipe," they are engaging in a symbolic gesture of harmony and mutual understanding, usually after a period of conflict or disagreement.

Origin

1. Native American Ceremonies: The phrase originates from the Native American custom of smoking a ceremonial pipe, often referred to as a "peace pipe," as a ritual to seal peace treaties or agreements between tribes or between tribes and European settlers. The act of sharing the pipe and its smoke was seen as a sacred and bonding experience.

2. Symbolism of Unity: The shared act of smoking the ceremonial pipe signified a coming together, a mutual respect, and a united front. The pipe itself, often intricately crafted and adorned, was not just a tool but a sacred object that represented the importance and solemnity of the agreements being made.

3. Cultural Appropriation and Misunderstanding: It's important to note that while the idiom has been widely used in English to mean "making peace," it can oversimplify and misrepresent the deeply cultural and spiritual significance of the original Native American practice. The phrase has been used in contexts far removed from its indigenous roots, sometimes leading to misunderstandings or misuse.

Example Sentence

"After years of rivalry, the two companies decided to smoke the peace pipe and collaborate on the new project."

The idiom "smoke the peace pipe" taps into the universal desire for harmony, reconciliation, and mutual understanding. However, while the phrase speaks to the broader human experience of conflict resolution, it's essential to approach its usage with respect and awareness, given its origins in specific cultural and spiritual practices of Native American peoples. Recognizing the depth and significance of the original customs can enrich our understanding of the idiom and promote a deeper appreciation for the diverse traditions that contribute to the tapestry of human expression.

Throw a Monkey Wrench

Meaning

The idiom "throw a monkey wrench" means to sabotage, disrupt, or cause complications in a plan, process, or operation. When someone "throws a monkey wrench," they introduce an element or obstacle that prevents things from going smoothly or as intended.

Origin

1. Tool Terminology: A monkey wrench is a type of adjustable wrench. Its name is believed to derive from its inventor, Charles Moncky, though this etymology is debated. Regardless of its naming origin, the monkey wrench is a tool used to grip and turn nuts and bolts.

2. From Utility to Sabotage: The transition from the tool's practical use to the figurative sense of causing disruption is a bit unclear. However, the visual imagery of literally throwing a tool into machinery provides a vivid depiction of abrupt disruption or breakdown, which likely led to the idiomatic usage.

3. Variations: In some parts, especially the UK, the phrase "throw a spanner in the works" is used with the same meaning. A spanner is the British term for what Americans typically call a wrench, and the idiom similarly evokes the image of machinery being abruptly halted by a foreign object.

Example Sentence

"We had everything planned for the event, but the sudden rainstorm threw a monkey wrench into our outdoor activities."

The idiom "throw a monkey wrench" underscores the unpredictability of plans and the challenges that can suddenly arise, hindering progress or intentions. It serves as a vivid reminder that, even with the best preparations, unforeseen obstacles can emerge, necessitating adaptability and resilience. The phrase aptly captures the essence of unexpected disruptions in various contexts, from personal plans to complex projects, emphasizing the value of being prepared for the unexpected.

Turn Over a New Leaf

Meaning

The idiom "turn over a new leaf" means to make a fresh start or to change one's behavior, attitude, or outlook for the better. When someone decides to "turn over a new leaf," they are committing to positive change or a new direction in their life.

Origin

1. Book Pages: The term "leaf" in this context refers to a page in a book, not a part of a plant. Historically, pages in books were often referred to as leaves. Turning over a new leaf would mean turning to a new page, which is blank and untouched, symbolizing a fresh start or a new chapter in one's life.

2. Historical Usage: The idiom has been in use since at least the 16th century. The metaphorical connection between turning a page and starting anew was a powerful and easily understood one, leading to its widespread usage and understanding.

3. Symbolism of Renewal: The act of turning a page, revealing a clean surface, mirrors the idea of leaving behind past mistakes or habits and embarking on a new journey or adopting a renewed mindset.

Example Sentence

"After years of struggling with bad habits, he decided to turn over a new leaf and lead a healthier lifestyle."

The idiom "turn over a new leaf" encapsulates the human desire for renewal, redemption, and self-improvement. It emphasizes the idea that individuals have the agency to change their path, make amends, and start afresh, no matter their past. The phrase is a testament to the resilience of the human spirit, underscoring the belief that it's never too late to change for the better and that everyone deserves the chance to rewrite their story.

Money and Wealth

Money Talks

The idiom "money talks" implies that money has power and influence. It suggests that those with wealth or financial resources can achieve more, get their way, or have a significant impact in various situations. The phrase often implies that money can influence decisions, sway opinions, or expedite processes in ways that other factors might not.

Origin

1. Historical Recognition of Wealth: Throughout history, wealth has been a symbol of power, influence, and prestige. Those with substantial financial resources have often been able to exert influence in politics, business, and personal matters. The recognition of this power likely led to the creation of the idiom.

2. Cultural Commentary: The phrase can be seen as both an acknowledgment of reality and a critique of society. While it recognizes the factual power of money, it also hints at the potentially corrupting influence of wealth and the moral questions surrounding decisions driven solely by financial considerations.

3. Modern Usage: The idiom has been in use in its current form since at least the 19th century, though the sentiment behind it is much older. The simplicity and directness of "money talks" have made it a widely recognized and frequently used phrase.

Example Sentence

"While many people voiced their concerns about the new development, the billionaire's investment seemed to silence the critics. As they say, money talks."

The idiom "money talks" serves as a concise reflection on the undeniable influence of wealth in various spheres of life. While it succinctly captures the power dynamics often seen in society, it also acts as a reminder and a critique of the potential pitfalls of decisions and systems driven purely by monetary considerations. The phrase urges introspection about the values that guide actions and the balance between financial interests and broader ethical considerations.

A Penny Saved is a Penny Earned

Meaning

The idiom "a penny saved is a penny earned" emphasizes the importance of saving money. It suggests that money that is saved or not spent is equivalent to money that is earned. In essence, being thrifty and managing your finances wisely is just as valuable as acquiring new income.

Origin

1. Historical Value of a Penny: Historically, a penny held significant value, and saving even small amounts of money was crucial for many people's livelihoods. Over time, the importance of this careful financial stewardship was encapsulated in this phrase.

2. Benjamin Franklin's Influence: While the sentiment behind the saying can be traced back much earlier, it is often attributed to Benjamin Franklin, who included a similar saying in his publication "Poor Richard's Almanack." Franklin's writings frequently emphasized thriftiness and wise money management.

3. Cultural Emphasis on Thrift: Throughout various cultures and historical periods, the value of saving money and living within one's means has been highlighted. This idiom reinforces the notion that accumulation of wealth isn't just about earning but also about effectively conserving what one already has.

Example Sentence

"Even though it might seem like a small amount now, remember that a penny saved is a penny earned, so it's worth putting aside."

The idiom "a penny saved is a penny earned" is a timeless reminder of the importance of financial prudence and the value of thrift. It speaks to the idea that sustainable wealth is not only about active acquisition but also about wise conservation. In an era of consumerism and instant gratification, the phrase stands as a counterpoint, urging individuals to consider the long-term benefits of saving and investing wisely.

Cash Cow

A "cash cow" refers to a business, product, or asset that consistently generates a steady flow of profits or cash, often requiring minimal reinvestment or effort to maintain its profitability. It's something that acts as a reliable source of income or benefits over time.

Origin

1. Agricultural Roots: The imagery evokes the idea of a dairy cow that, once acquired and cared for, can be milked on a regular basis to produce a steady supply of milk, which can then be sold for profit. Similarly, a business or product labeled as a "cash cow" continues to "produce" revenue without significant additional input.

2. Boston Consulting Group's Matrix: The term gained prominence in the business world from the Boston Consulting Group's Growth-Share Matrix, a strategic business analysis tool introduced in the 1970s. In this matrix, a "cash cow" is one of the four categories used to classify business units or products based on their market growth and market share. Cash cows have high market share in a slow-growing industry; thus they generate more cash than what can be invested in them in a meaningful way.

3. Common Business Parlance: Over time, the term moved beyond its specific use in the BCG matrix to become a part of common business parlance, representing any reliable and steady source of income.

Example Sentence

"The company's flagship software product has been a cash cow for years, consistently generating revenue even as they've introduced newer products."

The idiom "cash cow" underscores the value of steady, reliable profitability in the often unpredictable world of business. It highlights the importance of having assets or products that can be depended upon to generate revenue, allowing businesses to invest in riskier ventures or weather economic downturns. Whether referring to a bestselling book, a hit television show, or a popular service, "cash cow" emphasizes the sustained value and reliability of the asset in question.

Deep Pockets

The idiom "deep pockets" refers to someone who has substantial financial resources or wealth. When an individual or organization is described as having "deep pockets," it suggests that they have significant money to spend, invest, or allocate as they see fit.

Origin

1. Literal Imagery: The imagery of "deep pockets" is fairly straightforward. Pockets, being part of clothing, are used to hold and carry items. Deeper pockets would, logically, be able to hold more, just as a person with "deep pockets" metaphorically holds more wealth.

2. Historical Context: While it's unclear exactly when the phrase originated, the connection between the depth of one's pockets and their wealth or financial capacity is intuitive and has been part of English language idioms for a long time.

3. Modern Connotations: In contemporary usage, the term often goes beyond mere possession of wealth. It can imply the ability to fund large projects, weather financial downturns, or bear the brunt of financial liabilities. For instance, in legal contexts, someone with "deep pockets" might be targeted in lawsuits because they have the means to pay substantial damages.

Example Sentence

"The startup was eager to partner with the tech giant, knowing they had the deep pockets necessary to fund their ambitious projects."

The idiom "deep pockets" encapsulates the societal recognition and sometimes reverence of substantial financial capability. It's a recognition of the power and influence that comes with wealth, as well as the opportunities and security it can provide. The phrase serves as a shorthand for describing those who are not only wealthy but also financially potent and capable of significant economic undertakings.

Money Doesn't Grow on Trees

Meaning

The idiom "money doesn't grow on trees" is used to convey the idea that money is a limited resource and isn't easily obtained. It emphasizes the importance of hard work to earn money, the value of saving, and the need to be cautious with expenditures. It's often used as a reminder not to be wasteful or take money for granted.

Origin

1. Literal Interpretation: At face value, the phrase is a statement of fact. Money is not a natural resource that can be harvested like fruit from trees. This simple, evident truth is used metaphorically to convey the larger lesson about the value of money and the effort required to obtain it.

2. Historical Usage: The sentiment behind this saying has roots in many cultures, emphasizing hard work, thrift, and the finite nature of resources. The exact phrasing as "money doesn't grow on trees" has been popular in the English language for a few centuries.

3. Parental Guidance: This idiom has commonly been used by parents in various cultures and eras to teach their children about the value of money, the importance of budgeting, and the need to prioritize essential expenses.

Example Sentence

"When Jake asked for the third toy in a week, his mother reminded him that money doesn't grow on trees and that they had to be mindful of their spending."

The idiom "money doesn't grow on trees" is a timeless piece of wisdom emphasizing financial responsibility. It serves as a reminder that resources are limited, that we must work for our rewards, and that financial prudence is essential for long-term security and success. In an era where instant gratification is often sought, this saying underscores the virtues of patience, hard work, and wise financial stewardship.

Break the Bank

Meaning

The idiom "break the bank" refers to spending more money than one can afford or depleting one's financial resources. It can also imply a large expense or an endeavor that is particularly costly. The phrase is sometimes used more lightheartedly to describe something that is expensive but might not literally bankrupt someone.

Origin

1. Casino Origins: The term has origins in gambling, particularly in the game of Monte Carlo in the 19th century. If a player won more than the reserve of the gambling table, it was said that they "broke the bank." The casino would then use a ceremonial gesture of covering the table with a black cloth and reopening later with a replenished bank.

2. Symbolism of the Bank: The bank is traditionally seen as a place of financial stability and security. Thus, to "break" it would be to undermine or overwhelm that stability, suggesting a significant financial undertaking or loss.

3. Wider Cultural Usage: Over time, the phrase has been adapted into everyday language to describe any large expenditure or financial strain, not just those associated with gambling.

Example Sentence

"Julia wanted to have a lavish destination wedding, but she didn't want to break the bank, so she looked for cost-effective options to make her dream come true."

The idiom "break the bank" resonates with the common experiences of financial limitations and the challenges of budgeting. It's a reminder of the need for financial prudence and the consequences of overspending. Whether used in the context of personal finance, business decisions, or even playful banter about shopping or treating oneself, the phrase emphasizes the value and limitations of money.

Put Your Money Where Your Mouth Is

Meaning

The idiom "put your money where your mouth is" means to support one's stated opinion or belief by acting on it, rather than just talking or boasting. In essence, it's a challenge to prove the sincerity of one's beliefs by investing in them or taking a tangible action, often financially.

Origin

1. Literal Interpretation: The phrase combines the act of speaking (where your "mouth" is) with a tangible commitment (money). It implies that talk is cheap, and real commitment or belief is demonstrated through action, often by spending or risking one's own money.

2. Historical Usage: The idiom's exact origins are not definitively known, but its sentiment has been echoed throughout history in various cultures. The idea that actions speak louder than words is a universal theme.

3. Cultural Context: The phrase likely solidified in modern English during the 20th century, particularly in contexts where someone might boast about a particular investment, idea, or belief but hesitates to commit resources to it. It calls for tangible proof of commitment.

Example Sentence

"Everyone claims to care about the environment, but it's time for companies to put their money where their mouth is and invest in sustainable practices."

The idiom "put your money where your mouth is" emphasizes the dichotomy between words and actions. It challenges individuals, organizations, and even societies to move beyond mere rhetoric and demonstrate genuine commitment through tangible actions, especially when there's a cost or risk involved. It serves as a reminder that while words are important, it's actions, often with financial implications, that truly define our priorities and values.

In the Black

The idiom "in the black" refers to a financial state where an individual or organization is profitable or at least not in debt. It denotes positive finances, where revenues or assets exceed liabilities or expenses.

Origin

1. Ledger Origins: Historically, in financial ledgers and account books, positive amounts or profits were often written in black ink, while losses or debts were written in red ink. Being "in the black" would mean that the records were showing a profit rather than a loss.

2. Consistent Usage: The consistent use of black to represent profit and red for losses, especially in ledgers and balance sheets, has made the color symbolism relatively universal in the financial world.

3. Modern Financial Reporting: The concept has carried over into modern times, especially in business contexts. Companies aim to operate "in the black," particularly towards the end of the fiscal year, to demonstrate profitability.

Example Sentence

"After several years of struggling, the company finally turned things around and ended the year in the black."

The idiom "in the black" underscores the importance of profitability and fiscal responsibility in the business world. It's a universally recognized term signifying financial health and success. In a broader sense, it speaks to the positive outcomes that come from sound management, wise decision-making, and diligent effort. It's a goal that many businesses and individuals aspire to, highlighting the overarching value placed on financial stability and success.

Golden Handshake

A "golden handshake" refers to a large sum of money or a lucrative financial package offered to an executive or employee as an incentive for early retirement, resignation, or as compensation upon termination. It's often given to high-ranking executives by corporations as part of their employment contracts.

Origin

1. Terminology Origins: The term combines two symbolic words: "golden," implying something of great value, and "handshake," a gesture often associated with agreements or parting ways. When combined, they paint a picture of a valuable agreement or deal upon someone's departure from a company.

2. Business Practices: As businesses and corporations grew in size and complexity, particularly in the 20th century, contracts for top executives became more sophisticated. To either incentivize the departure of certain executives or to protect their financial interests upon termination, these large financial agreements (golden handshakes) became more common.

3. Public Awareness: High-profile cases of executives receiving large sums of money upon their departure from major companies have brought the term to public attention, often sparking debates on the ethics and appropriateness of such payouts, especially if a company is underperforming or facing scandals.

Example Sentence

"Despite the tech company's recent struggles, its outgoing CEO received a golden handshake worth millions."

The idiom "golden handshake" delves into the intricate world of corporate contracts and executive compensations. It's a reflection of the high stakes in corporate leadership roles and the complex nature of employment agreements at that level. While the term often carries a neutral or positive connotation in the business world, it can sometimes be viewed negatively by the general public, especially if perceived as excessive or unwarranted. It serves as a focal point in discussions about corporate responsibility, executive compensation, and business ethics.

Pinch Pennies

The idiom "pinch pennies" refers to the act of being very careful or frugal with money, often to the point of being overly cautious or stingy. It implies a strict adherence to saving and avoiding unnecessary expenditures.

Origin

1. Literal Interpretation: The imagery of "pinching" pennies suggests holding onto them so tightly that they might be pinched or squeezed. This visual helps emphasize the level of care or stinginess with which someone treats their money.

2. Historical Context: In times of economic hardships, such as the Great Depression, many individuals and families had to be extremely cautious with their finances, leading to a culture of saving every possible penny.

3. Coinage and Value: Historically, pennies (or small coins in many cultures) represented the smallest denomination of money. The act of being careful even with the smallest amount of money underscores a very detailed level of financial caution.

Example Sentence

"Even after winning the lottery, Jane continued to pinch pennies, always looking for the best deals and discounts."

The idiom "pinch pennies" captures the essence of frugality and the value some place on saving money, sometimes to an extreme degree. It's a testament to the notion that every little bit counts, especially when it comes to finances. The phrase can be used both admiringly, to denote wise financial prudence, and critically, to indicate excessive stinginess. It speaks to broader themes of financial management, the value of money, and cultural attitudes towards saving and spending.

Live High on the Hog

The idiom "live high on the hog" refers to living a luxurious or affluent lifestyle, enjoying the best of everything, particularly in terms of food and material comforts. Someone who "lives high on the hog" indulges in the finer things in life and has ample means to do so.

Origin

1. Culinary Roots: The term originates from the way meat is cut from a pig. The best and most tender cuts of meat, like pork loins and ham, come from the upper part or "high" on the hog, whereas the lower portions yield lesser cuts. Historically, those who could afford the better cuts were wealthier individuals, while the less affluent would often make do with the cheaper, tougher cuts from the lower part of the pig.

2. Cultural Context: In many cultures, the consumption of meat, especially choice cuts, has long been associated with wealth or celebratory occasions. Over time, this specific reference to pork became a metaphor for enjoying the best in life more generally.

3. Evolution of the Phrase: While the phrase began with a culinary connotation, it has since broadened to refer to luxury and affluence in all areas of life, not just in terms of food.

Example Sentence

"After his tech startup was acquired for billions, Mark started to live high on the hog, purchasing luxury cars and vacationing in exotic destinations."

The idiom "live high on the hog" encapsulates the human desire for luxury, comfort, and the finer things in life. It draws a direct link between material affluence and the quality of one's daily experiences, using the universal appreciation for good food as its base metaphor. The phrase can sometimes be used critically to suggest someone is living beyond their means or indulging excessively, but it can also be a neutral or positive acknowledgment of someone's success and ability to enjoy its fruits.

Money to Burn

Meaning

The idiom "money to burn" refers to having more money than one knows what to do with or having excessive funds that can be spent on non-essential items or activities without causing financial strain. It implies that someone is so wealthy that they could literally afford to waste money without concern.

Origin

1. Literal Interpretation: The visual imagery of burning money is powerful, suggesting wastefulness and excess. If someone had so much money that they could afford to literally set it on fire without worrying about the financial loss, it indicates great wealth.

2. Historical Uses: Though the precise origin of the phrase is unclear, the concept of conspicuous consumption—displaying wealth through wasteful extravagance—dates back centuries. The idiom "money to burn" aptly captures this notion of spending or using resources merely for the sake of display or indulgence.

3. Societal Observations: As societies moved into more capitalist and consumer-driven eras, displays of wealth became more common, and the idea of having "extra" money that could be freely spent (or even wasted) on luxuries became more prevalent.

Example Sentence

"With his recent lottery win, Jake acted like he had money to burn, buying extravagant gifts for everyone he knew."

The idiom "money to burn" touches on themes of wealth, excess, and the human tendency to showcase prosperity. It offers commentary on how people relate to money and the behaviors exhibited when financial constraints are removed. Whether used in admiration, envy, or criticism, the phrase underscores the complex emotions and societal judgments surrounding wealth and expenditure.

Rob Peter to Pay Paul

The idiom "rob Peter to pay Paul" describes a situation where one is solving a problem or settling a debt by creating another problem or debt. It implies a kind of zero-sum game where no real progress is made because taking from one source merely covers a shortfall in another.

Origin

1. Religious Foundations: One of the oldest theories about the origin of this phrase relates to religious institutions in London. St. Peter's was Westminster Abbey, and St. Paul's referred to the Cathedral. There were instances in history where funds allocated for the maintenance or repair of one church were said to be used for the other, leading to the perception that one was being "robbed" to benefit the other.

2. Broad Usage: While the exact origin remains debated, the phrase has been used in English since at least the 1300s. Its longevity suggests that the fundamental concept—solving one problem at the expense of creating another—has been a recurring theme throughout history.

3. Figurative Development: The names "Peter" and "Paul" in the idiom have likely become stand-ins for any two entities in a shifting balance of resources or favor. The specific names are less about the historical figures and more about the broader idea of taking from one to give to another.

Example Sentence

"Using your credit card to pay off a loan might feel like progress, but it's just robbing Peter to pay Paul."

The idiom "rob Peter to pay Paul" sheds light on the human tendency to seek quick fixes or shortcuts, even if they don't lead to genuine resolutions. It serves as a cautionary phrase, warning against solutions that may seem helpful in the short term but merely shift the problem elsewhere. The proverbial nature of the phrase emphasizes the universality of such dilemmas and encourages more holistic problem-solving approaches.

Filthy Rich

The idiom "filthy rich" refers to possessing immense wealth or being extremely wealthy. However, the term doesn't just highlight affluence; the word "filthy" often carries a negative connotation, implying that the wealth might be excessive, or even ill-gotten or undeserved.

Origin

1. Word Evolution: The word "filthy" has been used in English to mean "abundant" or "excessive" since at least the 1600s. Over time, this word, which typically refers to something unclean or dirty, began to be associated with the concept of excessive wealth.

2. Social Commentary: The term might have evolved as a form of social commentary. Extreme wealth, especially during periods of economic disparity, can sometimes be viewed with suspicion or disdain, leading to the idea that such wealth is "dirty" or corrupt.

3. Contrasting Imagery: The juxtaposition of "filthy," which often connotes something negative, with "rich," which is typically positive, creates a striking image. This contrast likely contributed to the phrase's popularity and longevity.

Example Sentence

"While many people in the town struggled to make ends meet, the industrial baron was filthy rich, with mansions across the country."

The idiom "filthy rich" encapsulates societal perceptions of immense wealth, especially when that wealth is deemed excessive or potentially unscrupulous. While the term can be used neutrally to simply denote great affluence, it often carries with it subtle (or not-so-subtle) judgments about the means by which that wealth was acquired or the way in which it's flaunted. The phrase taps into broader themes of wealth disparity, the ethics of accumulation, and societal values regarding money and success.

Make Ends Meet

The idiom "make ends meet" refers to having just enough money to cover one's expenses or bills without any left over. It emphasizes the act of managing one's finances such that income matches or barely exceeds expenses, often indicating a situation of financial tightness or struggle.

Origin

1. Nautical Origins: One theory posits that the phrase originates from the world of sailing. "Ends" in this context could refer to the ends of ropes. Making these rope ends meet would mean that everything was taut and in order, which could be a metaphor for financial stability.

2. Tailoring Origins: Another theory suggests the phrase comes from the tailoring world. When adjusting a garment, particularly in situations where fabric was scarce, a tailor had to ensure the "ends" (edges of the fabric) met precisely to make the piece of clothing fit.

3. General Usage Evolution: Regardless of its exact origin, by the 17th century, the phrase was used in its current figurative sense, indicating the balance of income and expenditure.

Example Sentence

"Since losing her job, Jane has been finding it increasingly hard to make ends meet, often juggling between paying bills and buying groceries."

The idiom "make ends meet" touches on themes of financial struggle, resourcefulness, and the universal human experience of trying to balance resources against needs. It encapsulates the challenge many face in trying to live within their means, especially in times of economic downturns or personal financial crises. The phrase serves as a testament to resilience and the tenacity many exhibit in navigating life's financial ups and downs.

Money Talks, Bullsh*t Walks

Meaning

This more colloquial idiom essentially means that money or financial power commands respect, results, or attention, whereas empty talk, false promises, or insincerity without financial backing or tangible action count for nothing. It underscores the idea that tangible resources (like money) are persuasive and influential, while mere words without backing are worthless.

Origin

1. Societal Commentary: This phrase seems to have originated in the 20th century and has been popularized in various forms in movies, music, and other media. It is a reflection of a capitalist society where money holds significant power and sway.

2. Juxtaposition for Emphasis: The stark contrast between "money" and "bullsh*t" in the idiom serves to emphasize the gap between action backed by tangible resources and empty promises or claims. By pairing these two concepts, the phrase delivers a clear and memorable message about the power of financial backing over mere talk.

3. Popularization in Media: The exact origin of the phrase is unclear, but its use in pop culture, movies, and music has ensured its place in contemporary English, particularly in American slang.

Example Sentence

"When the businessman promised to bring investments to the small town, the locals were skeptical. They believed in the principle that 'money talks, bullsh*t walks', and wanted to see actual funding before getting their hopes up."

The idiom "money talks, bullsh*t walks" carries a somewhat cynical view of the dynamics of power, influence, and trust in modern society. It underscores the notion that actions backed by tangible resources are more trustworthy and influential than mere words or promises. While the phrase is certainly direct and a bit crude, its bluntness captures the essence of its message, making it memorable and impactful.

Rolling in Dough

The idiom "rolling in dough" refers to having a substantial amount of money or being very wealthy. Someone who is "rolling in dough" is in a financially comfortable or even opulent situation.

Origin

1. Baking Imagery: The term "dough" has been slang for money for many years, and the act of "rolling" might be derived from the process of rolling out dough in baking. When you roll out dough, it expands, which could symbolically represent the expansion of wealth.

2. Slang Evolution: The word "dough" as a slang term for money has origins that date back to the 19th century in the United States. The association might come from the idea that money, like dough, can be shaped or molded to fit one's needs, or that money is a basic ingredient for many aspects of life, just as dough is a fundamental part of many foods.

3. Popular Usage: Over time, the phrase "rolling in dough" became a colorful and evocative way to describe someone with a lot of money, emphasizing not just wealth but an abundance or excess of it.

Example Sentence

"After his tech startup was acquired by a major corporation, Jake was suddenly rolling in dough and could afford luxuries he'd never even dreamed of."

The idiom "rolling in dough" paints a vivid picture of prosperity, using the tactile and familiar process of baking as a metaphor for financial success. It conveys not just the idea of wealth, but of abundance, luxury, and comfort. In a world where financial success is often aspired to and revered, this phrase offers a fun, informal way to describe the pinnacle of monetary achievement.

Cash-Strapped

Meaning

The idiom "cash-strapped" describes a situation or a person facing financial hardship or not having enough money to cover necessary expenses. Someone who is "cash-strapped" is in a tight or difficult financial situation.

Origin

1. Literal Imagery: The term combines "cash," referring to money, and "strapped," which can mean restricted, bound, or limited. The imagery suggests a binding or restriction due to a lack of funds.

2. Economic Context: This term has become more popular during economic downturns or recessions when many individuals, companies, or even governments face financial constraints.

3. Modern Usage: It's unclear when "cash-strapped" first emerged as a phrase, but its use has been prevalent in the 20th and 21st centuries, especially in journalistic contexts to describe entities facing financial challenges.

Example Sentence

"The cash-strapped student had to find a part-time job to afford his tuition fees."

The idiom "cash-strapped" succinctly captures the essence of financial constraint or hardship. It paints a clear picture of the pressure and limitations that come with not having enough money to meet one's needs or obligations. Especially relevant in times of economic challenge, the term has become a go-to descriptor for various entities, from individuals to large organizations, signaling the universality of financial struggles across different scales and contexts.

Money Can't Buy Happiness

The idiom "money can't buy happiness" conveys the idea that wealth and material possessions alone cannot guarantee or bring about true contentment, joy, or emotional and spiritual fulfillment. It underscores the belief that some of life's most valuable and enriching experiences are beyond the realm of monetary transactions.

Origin

1. Ancient Philosophical Roots: Philosophers, religious leaders, and thinkers throughout history have often extolled the virtues of non-materialistic pursuits. They've emphasized spiritual, emotional, and moral values over material possessions as sources of true contentment and meaning in life.

2. Literary References: The concept that money and material wealth are not the sole determinants of happiness has been a recurring theme in literature across cultures. Variations of this sentiment can be found in numerous writings, suggesting that the idea is ancient and universal.

3. Modern Usage: The exact phrasing "money can't buy happiness" became popular in the 19th and 20th centuries. The phrase has been used in songs, books, films, and speeches, further cementing its place in popular discourse.

Example Sentence

"While John had always dreamed of winning the lottery, once he did, he realized that money can't buy happiness, as he still felt a void in his life."

The idiom "money can't buy happiness" taps into the age-old debate about the role of material wealth in human well-being. While money can undoubtedly provide comfort, security, and access to many pleasures, the phrase serves as a reminder that intangible aspects of life, such as love, purpose, and inner peace, cannot be purchased. In an increasingly materialistic world, this saying acts as a counterpoint, urging individuals to seek balance and recognize the importance of non-materialistic sources of joy and contentment.

Nickel and Dime

Meaning

The idiom "nickel and dime" can be used in various contexts, but it generally refers to:

1. Small or insignificant amounts of money.
2. Being charged or subjected to many minor expenses, which can add up to a significant amount.
3. Petty or trivial matters.

When someone says they are being "nickel and dimed," they often mean they are being subjected to a series of small charges or expenses that, collectively, become burdensome or irritating.

Origin

1. U.S. Currency References: In the United States, the nickel and dime are among the lowest denominations of coins, representing five and ten cents respectively. Their low value makes them symbolic of small amounts or trivial matters.

2. Economic Usage: Over time, especially in the context of business and consumer experiences, the phrase began to be used to describe situations where multiple small charges or expenses accumulate, sometimes unfairly or unexpectedly.

3. Cultural Evolution: The idiom has been cemented in the language through its frequent use in literature, movies, and other forms of media where characters grapple with the pressures of numerous minor financial burdens.

Example Sentence

"After buying the printer at a discount, I felt nickel and dimed by the cost of ink cartridges and other accessories."

The idiom "nickel and dime" captures the frustrations and challenges of dealing with numerous small expenses or problems. In a broader sense, it speaks to the idea that many minor issues or costs, when combined, can have a significant impact. The phrase serves as a reminder to be vigilant of not just substantial singular costs or challenges but also the cumulative effect of multiple smaller ones.

124

Luck and Fate

The Luck of the Draw

The idiom "the luck of the draw" refers to outcomes determined by chance rather than by someone's actions or decisions. It suggests that the result of a particular situation was random and could not have been controlled or predicted.

Origin

1. Card Game Origins: This phrase likely has its roots in card games where players draw cards from a deck, and the outcome is based largely on chance rather than skill. In such games, getting a favorable or unfavorable card is often termed as the "luck of the draw."

2. Lotteries and Random Selection: The phrase also aligns with the concept of lotteries or other situations where outcomes are determined by a random draw or selection, emphasizing the role of luck or chance.

3. Broader Application: Over time, the phrase moved beyond just card games or lotteries and began to be used in a wide range of contexts to describe any situation where outcomes seem to be determined more by chance than by one's choices or actions.

Example Sentence

"Even with the best preparation, job interviews can be unpredictable. Sometimes it's just the luck of the draw whether you click with the interviewer or not."

The idiom "the luck of the draw" encapsulates the inherent uncertainties of life, where, despite our best efforts, outcomes can often be influenced by factors beyond our control. It serves as a reminder of the unpredictable nature of many situations and events, urging individuals to be resilient in the face of such uncertainties and to recognize that not all outcomes, good or bad, are a direct result of their actions.

Born with a Silver Spoon in One's Mouth

Meaning

The idiom "born with a silver spoon in one's mouth" refers to someone who is born into wealth and privilege. When this phrase is used, it suggests that the individual has been fortunate from birth, often inheriting advantages, opportunities, or wealth from their family without having had to earn them.

Origin

1. Historical Significance of Silver: Historically, silverware, especially silver spoons, was a sign of wealth and high social status. Such items were often passed down through generations as treasured family heirlooms.

2. Baptismal Tradition: There was a tradition in some cultures of gifting silver spoons to babies at their christening or baptism. Such a gift was usually given by those who could afford it, symbolizing a wish for prosperity for the child and also indicating the child's wealthy background.

3. Literary Usage: The phrase's popularity has been bolstered by its use in literature and other forms of media, where characters are often described as having been "born with a silver spoon" to highlight their privileged upbringings.

Example Sentence

"Jane never had to worry about finances or finding a job after college; she was born with a silver spoon in her mouth."

The idiom "born with a silver spoon in one's mouth" touches upon themes of privilege, inheritance, and the disparities that can exist from birth. It serves as a reminder of the socio-economic advantages that some individuals may have, not because of their efforts or merit but due to the circumstances of their birth. While the phrase often carries a slightly envious or critical tone, it underscores the broader discussions about wealth inequality and the role of privilege in shaping life outcomes.

Roll the Dice

The idiom "roll the dice" means to take a chance or a risk where the outcome is unpredictable. When someone decides to "roll the dice," they're making a decision or taking an action with uncertain consequences, hoping for a favorable result but acknowledging the inherent unpredictability.

Origin

1. Gaming Origins: The phrase directly originates from games of chance involving dice, such as craps. In these games, players roll dice to determine an outcome, and there's no way to predict the result, making it a gamble.

2. Cultural Evolution: Over time, the act of rolling dice in gaming came to symbolize risk-taking in broader contexts, moving beyond just games to refer to any situation where outcomes were uncertain.

3. Literary and Media Influence: The phrase's adoption and popularity have been facilitated by its use in literature, films, and other media forms where characters are faced with moments of decision that involve risk.

Example Sentence

"Instead of choosing a stable job, he decided to roll the dice and start his own business."

The idiom "roll the dice" encapsulates the universal theme of facing uncertainties in life. It resonates with the human experience of decision-making, where not all outcomes can be predicted or controlled. By choosing to "roll the dice," individuals embrace the unpredictable nature of certain situations, hoping for the best while being prepared for any outcome. The phrase serves as a reminder of the risks and rewards that come with making bold decisions and stepping into the unknown.

Knock on Wood

Meaning

The idiom "knock on wood," also known as "touch wood" in some cultures, is an expression people use to ward off bad luck or to hope that good luck continues after making a favorable statement about a situation. It is often accompanied by the gesture of physically knocking on a piece of wood.

Origin

1. Ancient Beliefs: The origins of this superstition are believed to date back to ancient times. Trees were often thought to house spirits or deities in various cultures. By knocking or touching wood, individuals might have been trying to call upon these spirits for protection or to ward off evil.

2. Christian Interpretation: Another theory suggests that the expression might have Christian roots, relating to the wood of the cross. Touching or knocking on wood in this context could be seen as a way to seek a blessing or protection from God.

3. Cultural Evolution: The idiom has persisted and evolved over time across various cultures, each with its own variations and interpretations. Its consistent presence in literature, folklore, and everyday conversations has solidified its place in modern vernacular.

Example Sentence

"I haven't been sick all year, knock on wood."

The idiom "knock on wood" touches upon the human tendency to rely on superstitions or rituals for comfort in uncertain situations. Whether it's out of genuine belief or just a habit, this expression and accompanying gesture serve as a symbolic means to hope for continued good fortune or to ward off potential misfortune. It's a reflection of the universal desire to influence outcomes and secure positive results, even if through seemingly inconsequential actions.

Horseshoe of Good Luck

The concept of a horseshoe as a symbol of good luck is rooted in various folklore and superstitions. Many believe that hanging a horseshoe over a doorway or having one in possession can bring good fortune, ward off evil, and protect against negative energies or occurrences.

Origin

1. Ancient Protection: Horseshoes, made of iron, were believed to ward off evil spirits in ancient times. Iron was considered a magical material that could deter malevolent forces or beings.

2. Saint Dunstan: A popular legend attributes the horseshoe's lucky properties to Saint Dunstan, a historical figure who lived in England during the 10th century. As the story goes, Dunstan, who was a blacksmith, was visited by the Devil. He managed to shoe the Devil's hoof, causing him great pain. The Devil agreed to never enter a home adorned with a horseshoe in exchange for Dunstan's promise to remove the shoe.

3. Orientation Matters: There are differing opinions on the correct way to hang a horseshoe for good luck. Some believe it should be hung with the open end up so that the luck doesn't spill out, while others think it should be hung with the open end down, allowing the luck to pour onto those who pass beneath.

Example Sentence

"Ever since grandma hung that old horseshoe of good luck above the front door, she swears the house has felt more peaceful and prosperous."

The concept of the "horseshoe of good luck" underscores the human penchant for finding symbols and rituals to attract positivity or ward off negativity. Across cultures and generations, people have sought tangible objects to represent abstract ideas of luck, protection, and prosperity. The horseshoe stands as a testament to such traditions, serving as both a cultural relic and a continuing symbol of hope and fortune.

On the Cards

The idiom "on the cards" implies that something is likely to happen or is expected to take place. It's used to refer to a situation or event that is anticipated or seen as a probable occurrence.

Origin

1. Card Games and Fortune-Telling: The origin of the phrase is believed to be connected to the world of card games and, more specifically, to cartomancy—the practice of fortune-telling using a deck of cards. Just as a card reader might predict future events by interpreting a spread of cards, the phrase came to symbolize something that is foreseen or expected.

2. Evolution of Usage: The idiom was used more broadly over time, moving away from just the literal act of card-based predictions to denote any event or situation that seemed likely to happen.

3. Variations: In American English, the phrase "in the cards" is more commonly used, while "on the cards" is predominantly a British English expression.

Example Sentence

"With the way the team has been performing recently, a championship win seems on the cards."

The idiom "on the cards" taps into the age-old human fascination with prediction and foretelling. Whether through divination methods like tarot cards or simply observing patterns and trends in everyday life, people have always sought ways to anticipate future events. This phrase captures that sentiment, hinting at the inevitable or expected, often with an air of resignation or acceptance of what's to come. It's a reminder that while we might hope or plan for certain outcomes, there are aspects of the future we see as almost predestined or highly probable.

Wish Upon a Star

Meaning

The idiom "wish upon a star" refers to the act of making a wish with the hopeful expectation that it will come true, even if the chances are slim. It emphasizes optimism, dreams, and the belief in possibilities beyond the ordinary. The expression is often associated with a sense of wonder and the innocence of childhood.

Origin

1. Ancient Astral Beliefs: For millennia, humans have looked to the stars with awe and reverence. Many ancient cultures believed that stars had divine or mystical properties. Wishing upon a star could have been seen as a way to communicate one's desires to the heavens or divine entities.

2. Popular Culture: The phrase was popularized in Western culture, in part, by the song "When You Wish Upon a Star," written by Leigh Harline and Ned Washington for Walt Disney's 1940 adaptation of Pinocchio. The song's lyrics convey the idea that dreams can come true if you wish upon a star, cementing the phrase's association with hope and magic.

3. Symbolism of Stars: Stars are often seen as distant, untouchable, and mysterious, making them perfect symbols for dreams and wishes that might seem unattainable.

Example Sentence

"Even though the odds were against her, she decided to wish upon a star and pursue her dream of becoming a renowned artist."

The idiom "wish upon a star" encapsulates the perennial human tendency to dream and hope against all odds. It's a beautiful reflection of the optimism that often characterizes the human spirit. Whether through ancient practices of stargazing or through modern tales of magic and wonder, this phrase serves as a timeless reminder of the importance of dreams and the power of hope. It suggests that no matter how distant or improbable a desire may seem, there's always a glimmer of possibility if one holds onto their dreams.

Stroke of Luck

Meaning

The idiom "stroke of luck" refers to an unexpected or sudden fortunate event or occurrence. It's used to describe a lucky incident that happens by chance rather than as a result of one's own actions or efforts.

Origin

1. Literal Interpretation: The word "stroke" in this context can be understood as something that happens swiftly or suddenly, similar to how one might strike swiftly with a brush or hand. Combining this with "luck" gives the impression of a rapid, unforeseen turn of good fortune.

2. Use Over Time: While the exact origins of the phrase are not definitively documented, its use in literature and everyday language has been consistent over time, solidifying its place in the English language.

3. Cultural Context: The idea of attributing good fortune to chance or external forces is common across many cultures, and in English, this sentiment is captured succinctly with the phrase "stroke of luck."

Example Sentence

"When she found a rare coin on the street worth thousands, she realized it was truly a stroke of luck."

The idiom "stroke of luck" taps into the universal human experience of encountering unexpected good fortune. Throughout life, there are moments where serendipity or pure chance seems to favor an individual, often in surprising ways. This phrase captures those moments, emphasizing the unpredictable nature of luck. It's a reminder that, despite our best plans and efforts, there are always elements of randomness and unpredictability in life that can work in our favor. Whether it's finding a lost item, meeting a helpful stranger, or dodging a potential misfortune, a "stroke of luck" celebrates those fortuitous moments that make life's journey all the more intriguing.

Cross One's Fingers

The idiom "cross one's fingers" is used to express the hope that something will happen in a good way or as desired. It can also be used to wish someone else luck. Additionally, the physical act of crossing one's middle finger over the index finger is a common gesture associated with hoping for good luck.

Origin

1. Pagan Rituals: The gesture of crossing fingers is believed to date back to pre-Christian times in Europe. Pagans would cross their fingers to invoke the power of a protective spirit or to ward off evil. The intersection of the fingers symbolized unity and the benign spirits that resided at crossroads or intersections.

2. Christian Context: With the spread of Christianity, the gesture began to be associated with the Christian cross. Crossing fingers became a covert way for Christians to bless themselves or to pray for protection during times of persecution.

3. Two-Person Gesture Evolution: It's thought that in early practices, one person would make a wish and another person would cross their index finger over the wisher's finger to support the wish. Over time, this evolved into the single-person gesture we recognize today.

4. Modern Use: In modern times, while the gesture retains its association with hoping for luck or favorable outcomes, it's also sometimes used to excuse a small lie or breach of promise. For instance, one might cross their fingers behind their back to indicate that they're not entirely truthful.

Example Sentence

"He was nervous about the interview, so he crossed his fingers hoping it would go well."

The idiom "cross one's fingers" encapsulates a universal desire for good outcomes and a touch of superstition. Over time, as the gesture evolved from religious and pagan origins to secular use, it remained a symbol of hope and wishful thinking. In moments of uncertainty or anticipation, it's a small act that offers comfort, illustrating the deeply human need for positive reinforcement, even if it comes from our own subtle gestures.

Fate is Sealed

Meaning

The idiom "fate is sealed" conveys the idea that an outcome or consequence has been determined and is inevitable. It's often used in situations where events have been set in motion that cannot be undone or altered, leading to a particular outcome or destiny.

Origin

1. Ancient Practices of Sealing Documents: Historically, important documents were sealed with wax to keep them secure and confidential. Once the seal was set, it served two purposes: to protect the document from being tampered with and to authenticate its source. Breaking the seal without proper authority was a breach of trust or even illegal. Thus, when a seal was placed on a document, the contents and decisions within that document became final.

2. Fate and Destiny in Literature and Mythology: The concept of a predetermined fate or destiny is ancient and can be found in many cultures' mythologies and literature. The idea that once certain events are set into motion they can't be changed is a recurring theme. Combining the finality of a seal with the concept of fate makes this idiom powerful in its representation.

3. Judicial and Royal Decrees: In historical contexts, when a king or a judicial body made a decision and sealed it with their official seal, it symbolized that the decision was final and not open to appeal or alteration.

Example Sentence

"After the jury gave its verdict, it felt like his fate was sealed."

The idiom "fate is sealed" taps into the profound human emotion associated with inevitability. When circumstances seem out of our control, this phrase succinctly captures the feeling of resignation to an impending outcome. Whether it's used in the context of personal decisions, legal situations, or historical events, "fate is sealed" reminds us of the moments in life when the trajectory seems set, challenging us to either accept the inevitable or find resilience in the face of it.

Break a Leg

The idiom "break a leg" is a colloquial expression of good luck, especially in the world of theater and performances. Ironically, instead of wishing someone good luck directly, a seemingly inauspicious wish is given. It's most commonly used before someone is about to perform, such as before an actor goes on stage, but it can also be used in other contexts to wish someone success.

Origin

1. Superstition in the Theatre: In the world of theater, there are many superstitions. One of them is the belief that directly wishing someone "good luck" would bring them bad luck. Therefore, an alternative way to wish luck was developed – by hoping for the exact opposite, like breaking a leg.

2. Origins in Vaudeville: Another theory suggests that in vaudeville (a type of theatrical variety show), performers only got paid if they performed on stage. Thus, "break a leg" referred to breaking the visual "line" of the stage, ensuring that one would indeed get a chance to perform and thus get paid.

3. Reference to Curtains: The legs are also the name for the curtains on the sides of a proscenium stage. Therefore, "break a leg" might mean making such a strong impression that the performance would warrant a curtain call, requiring the curtains or "legs" to be "broken" or parted.

Example Sentence

"As the lead actress prepared for her debut, the director shouted, 'Break a leg!' from offstage."

The idiom "break a leg" is a testament to the quirky and superstitious nature of show business. It serves as a reminder of the traditions, rituals, and beliefs that performers and artists have held onto for generations. Rather than a direct wish of good fortune, "break a leg" provides an indirect, yet heartfelt, sentiment of encouragement and hope for a successful performance. Over time, the saying has transcended theater and found its way into other domains, where it continues to bring a touch of theatrical flair to well-wishes.

Throw Caution to the Wind

The idiom "throw caution to the wind" means to act recklessly or take risks without considering the consequences. When someone "throws caution to the wind," they are choosing to behave in a manner that disregards potential dangers or repercussions in favor of pursuing an action or goal.

Origin

1. Nautical Origins: The phrase is believed to have nautical roots. In the context of sailing, wind direction and strength are crucial factors for navigation and safety. If a sailor were to ignore these elements (i.e., "throwing caution to the wind"), it would mean they are taking considerable risks.

2. Literal Interpretation: The act of throwing something into the wind means it can be blown back into one's face. Hence, disregarding caution might result in immediate repercussions, emphasizing the risks involved in such behavior.

3. Usage Evolution: Over time, the phrase transitioned from its possible maritime origins to more general use. It began to represent any scenario where an individual or group disregards potential dangers in pursuit of their objectives, whether it be in business, personal decisions, or other adventures.

Example Sentence

"Knowing the risks of the investment, Jane decided to throw caution to the wind and put her savings into the venture."

The idiom "throw caution to the wind" embodies the human spirit of adventure and risk-taking. While caution and prudence are often advocated in many situations, there are moments when the allure of potential gains or the thrill of the unknown prompts individuals to act boldly. This phrase encapsulates that sentiment, reminding us of the inherent risks but also celebrating the audacity to step outside of one's comfort zone. Whether driven by ambition, passion, or sheer impulsiveness, "throwing caution to the wind" is a testament to the lengths individuals will go to chase their dreams or desires.

On a Wing and a Prayer

Meaning

The idiom "on a wing and a prayer" refers to someone continuing to hope and persevere through a difficult or uncertain situation, even though success seems unlikely. It can also be used to describe advancing or progressing through something with a minimal chance of success, often relying on hope or sheer will rather than concrete means or solutions.

Origin

1. World War II Influence: This phrase became popular during World War II, primarily due to a patriotic song titled "Comin' in on a Wing and a Prayer" by Harold Adamson and Jimmie McHugh. The song tells the story of a damaged warplane, barely able to fly, attempting to return to its home base.

2. Air Combat and Bombing Runs: The idiom captures the essence of wartime aerial combat, especially during WWII when planes would often return from bombing runs with significant damage. The hope of these brave pilots and crew members was that they could land safely, even if the odds were against them—hence the reliance on a "wing and a prayer."

3. Evolution of Usage: Over time, the phrase transcended its wartime roots to be used in broader contexts. While it initially depicted the literal scenario of aircraft making it back in adverse conditions, it later came to symbolize any situation where success seemed improbable, but hope remained.

Example Sentence

"With barely any resources and a looming deadline, the team finished the project on a wing and a prayer."

The idiom "on a wing and a prayer" resonates with the human spirit of resilience, hope, and determination. It captures the essence of pressing on in the face of adversity, often against the odds. This phrase serves as a reminder of the indomitable will that people can exhibit, especially when backed into a corner or faced with challenging scenarios. Whether referencing its historical roots or more metaphorical undertakings, "on a wing and a prayer" evokes a sense of gritty perseverance combined with a touch of hopeful optimism.

Pot of Gold at the End of the Rainbow

Meaning

The idiom "pot of gold at the end of the rainbow" refers to a grand but elusive treasure or reward that one seeks, often in vain. It signifies an unattainable or fanciful goal that remains just out of reach, regardless of the efforts put in to achieve it. It can also be used to describe a distant or unlikely dream that people chase, believing it holds immense promise or fortune.

Origin

1. Irish Folklore: The idea of a pot of gold at the end of the rainbow finds its roots in Irish folklore. According to legend, leprechauns—mischievous fairies in Irish mythology—would bury pots filled with gold coins at the end of the rainbow to hide them from humans. However, since a rainbow's end cannot be reached (due to the optical nature of rainbows), the treasure remains forever elusive.

2. Symbolic Representation: The rainbow itself is a beautiful but fleeting natural phenomenon, and its elusive nature complements the idea of an unattainable or ever-shifting goal. The vibrant spectrum of colors ending in a promised treasure paints a picture of hope, dreams, and the pursuit of the unattainable.

3. Cultural Influence: The image of this pot of gold has been popularized in various forms of media, from songs and stories to movies, reinforcing the idea of chasing dreams or treasures that are just beyond one's grasp.

Example Sentence

"Many people move to Hollywood, seeing it as the pot of gold at the end of the rainbow, only to realize how challenging the entertainment industry can be."

The idiom "pot of gold at the end of the rainbow" encapsulates the eternal human pursuit of dreams, ambitions, and desires. It underscores the allure of the unattainable and the lengths to which individuals might go in the hope of achieving their goals. At the same time, it offers a cautionary reminder about the ephemeral and often elusive nature of such pursuits. Whether one is chasing dreams, wealth, or happiness, this phrase serves as a poetic representation of both the journey and the ever-distant destination.

Star-Crossed Lovers

Meaning

The term "star-crossed lovers" refers to a pair of lovers whose relationship is thwarted by external forces, often leading to tragedy. It implies that the stars, or fate, are against their relationship, suggesting an element of predestined misfortune or ill luck. The term often emphasizes a strong romantic love that faces various challenges and is frequently used to describe couples whose love story ends in sorrow or heartbreak.

Origin

1. Shakespearean Influence: The phrase is most famously associated with William Shakespeare's play "Romeo and Juliet," where it appears in the prologue: "From forth the fatal loins of these two foes / A pair of star-cross'd lovers take their life." The phrase describes the ill-fated love of Romeo and Juliet, who come from feuding families and whose relationship ends tragically.

2. Astrological Beliefs: In Elizabethan times, and long before, many people believed in the influence of stars and planets on human affairs. To be "star-crossed" was to be opposed by the stars, which often played a role in determining one's fate or destiny. The idea that the alignment or position of celestial bodies could dictate one's luck or future was prevalent.

3. Literary and Cultural Evolution: After Shakespeare, the concept of "star-crossed lovers" persisted in literature, art, and popular culture. The term became synonymous with lovers who face insurmountable challenges, often with tragic outcomes.

Example Sentence

"Despite their deep love for each other, political unrest meant that they were star-crossed lovers, forever kept apart by the turmoil of their nations."

The idiom "star-crossed lovers" encapsulates the profound and timeless theme of love facing adversity. It speaks to the universal human experiences of love, fate, and the challenges that sometimes stand in the way of love's fulfillment. The phrase serves as a poignant reminder of the fragile nature of romantic relationships, especially when they're up against societal, familial, or other external pressures. The story of Romeo and Juliet, emblematic of this phrase, continues to resonate because it captures the heartbreak of love that, due to circumstances beyond one's control, can't find its happy ending.

Swim Against the Tide

Meaning

The idiom "swim against the tide" refers to acting in opposition to a prevailing trend or taking a stance contrary to the majority. It denotes a challenge or resistance to the dominant viewpoint or the mainstream way of doing things. This phrase often implies that the individual or group is making a deliberate choice that may be difficult, unpopular, or even counterproductive, yet they persevere despite the odds or opposition.

Origin

1. Natural Observation: The phrase is derived from the literal observation of fish or swimmers trying to move upstream or against the current in a body of water. Going against the tide or current is noticeably more challenging than moving with it.

2. Symbolism of Water: Throughout history, water currents and tides have been symbolic of powerful forces, both natural and societal. To attempt to swim against such a force symbolizes a significant effort or struggle against something much larger than oneself.

3. Cultural References: Over time, the phrase has been employed metaphorically in literature, speeches, and everyday language to denote resistance or opposition to prevailing trends or opinions. It embodies the spirit of individualism and the courage of convictions, even in the face of adversity.

Example Sentence

"Although most of the industry was adopting the new technology, Jenna decided to swim against the tide and stick with the traditional methods that she believed in."

The idiom "swim against the tide" encapsulates the essence of determination, resilience, and courage. It speaks to the universal human experience of facing and challenging the status quo, societal norms, or popular opinion. The phrase serves as a metaphorical representation of the inner strength and conviction required to uphold one's beliefs and values, even when it seems the whole world is moving in a different direction. Whether it's a decision in business, personal life, or societal matters, "swim against the tide" is a tribute to those who dare to be different and are unafraid to chart their own course.

A Lucky Break

The idiom "a lucky break" refers to an unexpected event or situation that results in an advantage or opportunity for someone. It often implies a stroke of good fortune that comes unexpectedly, helping one to advance, succeed, or get out of a difficult situation.

Origin

1. Literal Interpretation: The word "break" has various meanings, and in the context of this idiom, it can be thought of as an opportunity or opening. Combining it with "lucky" emphasizes the fortuitous nature of the event.

2. Sports and Games: One possible origin ties to games like billiards or pool where a "break" is the first shot to scatter the balls, and a good break might set the player up for a successful game. A "lucky break" in this context would refer to an especially advantageous initial shot, largely attributed to luck rather than skill.

3. Entertainment Industry: The phrase is also commonly used in the entertainment industry, where newcomers might get a "big break" or "lucky break" — an unforeseen opportunity that launches their career.

Example Sentence

"After months of searching for a job, Jake got a lucky break when he ran into an old classmate who was starting a new company and needed his expertise."

The idiom "a lucky break" emphasizes the unpredictable nature of life and the role of serendipity in shaping our paths. While skill, dedication, and hard work are crucial components of success, this phrase acknowledges that sometimes unforeseen circumstances, chance encounters, or even plain luck can have a significant impact on our trajectories. It's a reminder that while we strive for success and navigate challenges, there might be unexpected turns of events that can offer us advantages or new possibilities.

The Die is Cast

The idiom "the die is cast" signifies that a decision has been made or an action has been taken that is irrevocable, and its consequences are now inevitable. Once the "die" (singular of "dice") is thrown, the result cannot be changed, mirroring situations in life where certain actions can't be taken back.

1. Ancient Rome: The phrase is often attributed to Julius Caesar. As he crossed the Rubicon River with his troops in 49 BC, effectively declaring war against the Roman Senate, he is believed to have said "Alea iacta est," which translates from Latin to "The die is cast." Crossing the Rubicon was considered an act of treason, so Caesar's decision was irreversible, and a turning point in Roman history.

2. Gaming and Dice: The analogy draws from the unpredictability of throwing dice. Once dice are thrown in a game, players must accept the outcome, whether it's favorable or not. Similarly, certain decisions in life lead to outcomes that must be faced, regardless of whether they are positive or negative.

"After years of hesitation, Marie finally decided to quit her stable job and start her own business. The die is cast, and she's now fully committed to her new journey."

The idiom "the die is cast" encapsulates the gravity of crucial decisions and the point of no return that often accompanies them. It resonates with moments in our lives when we're faced with choices that will change the course of our future, for better or for worse. The phrase serves as a reminder of the weight and finality of some decisions, prompting reflection and consideration before taking significant actions. It also conveys a sense of resolution and determination, urging one to embrace the consequences of their choices, whatever they may be.

A Roll of the Dice

Meaning

The idiom "a roll of the dice" refers to an action or decision that has an unpredictable outcome or involves taking a risk. Similar to the act of rolling dice in a game, where the outcome is uncertain, this phrase emphasizes the element of chance and the unknown.

Origin

1. Gaming Origins: Dice games have been played for millennia across various cultures. The unpredictability inherent in rolling dice — not knowing which numbers will face up — is a primary feature of many games. This uncertainty and reliance on luck translate easily into real-life scenarios where outcomes are not guaranteed.

2. Risk and Chance: In many cultures, dice have become synonymous with taking risks or gambling. Whether it's a simple game or more complex gambling scenarios, the roll of dice often determines wins and losses, mirroring the unpredictability of certain life decisions.

Example Sentence

"Starting a new business in such a volatile market feels like a roll of the dice, but I'm willing to take the chance."

The idiom "a roll of the dice" encapsulates the essence of venturing into the unknown and taking risks. It underscores the reality that not all outcomes can be foreseen or controlled. This phrase reminds us that, just as in games, life involves moments of unpredictability where we must rely on a mix of preparation, strategy, and sometimes just plain luck. It resonates with those moments of uncertainty, urging individuals to weigh the potential risks and rewards before making significant decisions. At the same time, it also celebrates the boldness of taking chances and embracing the unpredictability of life.

Play the Hand You're Dealt

Meaning

The idiom "play the hand you're dealt" suggests accepting and making the best of one's current circumstances, even if they are not ideal or what one hoped for. It derives from card games, where players must strategize with the cards they receive, regardless of whether they are good or bad.

Origin

1. Card Games: In many card games, players do not have control over the cards they are dealt. Instead, they must strategize and make decisions based on the hand they receive. This unpredictability and reliance on strategic play regardless of the initial hand mirrors the challenges faced in life where individuals have to make the best out of sometimes unfavorable situations.

2. Life's Unpredictability: Just as in card games, people often encounter situations in life that are unexpected or beyond their control. The concept of playing one's hand signifies facing these challenges head-on and trying to make the best of them, even if the initial conditions aren't ideal.

Example Sentence

"Even though he grew up in a challenging environment, Robert chose to play the hand he was dealt, working hard and eventually establishing a successful business."

The idiom "play the hand you're dealt" resonates with the universal experience of facing unforeseen challenges and the human capacity for resilience and adaptability. It's a call to action, encouraging individuals not to be deterred by initial setbacks or unfavorable circumstances but instead to find ways to navigate and make the most of them. It speaks to the human spirit's tenacity, emphasizing that while we might not always have control over the situations we find ourselves in, we can always control our reactions and decisions in response to them.

Food and Drink

In a Pickle

The idiom "in a pickle" refers to someone being in a difficult, challenging, or tricky situation. It's used to describe times when a person finds themselves in a predicament or quandary, uncertain about how to proceed or resolve the issue.

Origin

1. Shakespearean Roots: One of the earliest known uses of the phrase "in a pickle" comes from William Shakespeare's play "The Tempest" (1611). In Act 5, Scene 1, the character Trinculo states, "I have been in such a pickle since I saw you last." While the context in the play doesn't perfectly align with the modern usage, it still suggests a state of disarray or intoxication.

2. Dutch Influence: The term "pickle" comes from the Dutch word "pekel," which means a solution, such as brine, used to preserve food. Over time, "pickle" came to represent the finished product, i.e., vegetables (like cucumbers) preserved in a vinegar solution. The process of pickling can be seen as transformative, changing something from its original state into something quite different – perhaps analogous to someone finding themselves transformed from a state of normalcy into a problematic situation.

3. Possible Nautical Links: There's also a suggestion that the phrase might have nautical origins. A "pickle" was a colloquial term for the solution in which sailors preserved meat. Being "in the pickle" might have referred to meat being immersed in the solution, drawing a parallel to someone being deep in trouble.

Example Sentence

"After misplacing the event tickets, Jane found herself in a pickle, not knowing how to tell her friends about the oversight."

The phrase "in a pickle" paints a vivid image of someone immersed in a challenging or uncomfortable situation, much like cucumbers submerged in a pickling solution. It's a colorful way to convey the feeling of being trapped or stuck, seeking a way out of an unpleasant circumstance. The idiom serves as

Spill the Beans

Meaning

The idiom "spill the beans" means to reveal a secret or divulge confidential information, either accidentally or intentionally.

Origin

1. Ancient Voting: One theory suggests that this phrase originates from ancient Greece, where people would cast votes using beans. Placing a white bean in the container indicated a positive vote, while a black bean indicated a negative one. If the container was accidentally knocked over and the beans were spilled, the results would be revealed prematurely.

2. Agricultural Setting: Another theory posits that the phrase has agricultural roots, referring to the act of tipping over a container, causing beans to spill and scatter, revealing its contents.

Example Sentence

"During the team meeting, Jake accidentally spilled the beans about the upcoming product launch, much to everyone's surprise."

The idiom "spill the beans" captures the essence of unintentionally revealing something meant to be kept hidden. It suggests that, just as beans scatter unpredictably when spilled, secrets can get out in ways that are unexpected and uncontrollable. This phrase is often used in contexts where information was meant to be confidential or a surprise but becomes public knowledge due to a slip of the tongue or oversight. It underscores the idea that secrets are delicate and can be challenging to contain, serving as a reminder of the caution needed when handling sensitive information. Whether in personal relationships, professional environments, or casual conversations, "spill the beans" resonates with the sometimes unintended consequences of sharing information.

In a Nutshell

The idiom "in a nutshell" is used to indicate that someone is expressing something in a very concise way or summarizing a complex idea in a few words. When someone uses this phrase, they're often about to provide a short explanation or summary of a longer topic.

Origin

1. Classical Literature: The origins of this idiom can be traced back to classical times. There's a legend that the ancient Roman author Pliny the Elder mentioned that a copy of Homer's "Iliad" was small enough to be enclosed in a walnut shell. Whether or not such a tiny copy actually existed is debatable, but the idea of something vast being reduced to such a small size left an impact.

2. Symbolism of a Nutshell: Nutshells are compact, protective casings for seeds. The imagery of condensing a large amount of information or a complex idea into a small space, like a nutshell, is powerful and memorable.

Example Sentence

"The novel spans multiple generations and continents, but in a nutshell, it's about the enduring power of love and family."

The idiom "in a nutshell" encapsulates the concept of brevity and clarity in communication. It speaks to the skill of distilling complex ideas into their essential elements, making them more accessible and easy to understand. This phrase reminds listeners or readers that they are getting a summarized version, encouraging them to delve deeper if they wish to grasp the full picture. It emphasizes the importance of concise expression, especially in a world inundated with information. Whether used in presentations, discussions, or everyday conversation, "in a nutshell" signals a quick encapsulation of a topic, ensuring the listener's understanding without getting lost in extensive details.

Piece of Cake

Meaning

The idiom "piece of cake" is used to describe something that is very easy or uncomplicated to accomplish. When someone says a task is a "piece of cake," they mean that it requires little effort to complete.

Origin

1. American Slang: The phrase is believed to have originated in the U.S. during the 20th century, becoming popular slang by the 1940s. While the exact origins are unclear, it's likely tied to the pleasantness and simplicity associated with eating a slice of cake.

2. Related Expressions: Other similar idioms that use food or dessert imagery to convey ease include "easy as pie" and "cherry on top." The act of eating a dessert like cake or pie is often seen as enjoyable and effortless, hence the association with tasks that are easy to complete.

Example Sentence

"I was worried about the exam, but after studying, it turned out to be a piece of cake."

The idiom "piece of cake" plays on the universally relatable joy of indulging in a sweet treat. It taps into the idea that just as enjoying a slice of cake is straightforward and delightful, certain tasks or challenges can be straightforward and easily manageable. This phrase is often employed to instill confidence or to downplay the complexity of a task. It's a reminder that with the right approach or preparation, challenges that might seem daunting at first can turn out to be quite simple. Whether it's used in casual conversation, educational settings, or professional environments, "piece of cake" offers a lighthearted way to express the ease of an undertaking.

Couch Potato

The idiom "couch potato" refers to a person who leads a sedentary lifestyle, especially one who spends a lot of time watching television or engaging in other passive activities while sitting or lying down. It denotes laziness, inactivity, and a lack of physical exercise.

Origin

1. Television Era: The term came into use during the 1970s, coinciding with the rise of television as a dominant form of entertainment. As more households acquired TVs and broadcasting hours extended, many people began spending increased amounts of time in front of their screens.

2. Etymological Roots: The "couch" part of the term references the furniture piece on which one might lounge while watching TV. The "potato" aspect is a bit more metaphorical. Potatoes are tubers that remain underground (static and out of sight) as they grow, making them an apt symbol for inactivity.

Example Sentence

"Ever since he got that new gaming console, he's turned into a real couch potato."

The idiom "couch potato" evokes an image of lethargy and complacency, capturing a snapshot of modern sedentary lifestyles. It serves as a light-hearted critique of the inertia that can come with overindulgence in passive entertainment, warning of the potential health and social implications of such a lifestyle. In an age where screen-based activities (from television to computers to smartphones) are prevalent, "couch potato" is a reminder of the importance of balance, physical activity, and engagement with the world beyond our screens. The phrase humorously encourages individuals to be mindful of the time they spend inactive and to seek more active and diverse forms of recreation and relaxation.

Apple of My Eye

Meaning

The idiom "apple of my eye" is used to describe someone who is cherished deeply and held in very high regard. It often refers to someone's favorite person, usually someone they care for deeply, such as a child, partner, or close friend.

Origin

1. Ancient Texts: The phrase has origins that can be traced back to ancient times. One of the earliest uses is found in the Bible, specifically in the Book of Psalms (Psalm 17:8): "Keep me as the apple of the eye, hide me under the shadow of thy wings."

2. Biological Reference: In Old English, the pupil of the eye (the central and most important part) was referred to as the "apple". It was believed to be a solid, round object, hence the comparison to an apple. Protecting the pupil is essential for maintaining vision, so referring to it in such a manner emphasized its importance. Over time, this idea of preciousness and protection extended metaphorically to loved ones.

Example Sentence

"My granddaughter is the apple of my eye; there's nothing I wouldn't do for her."

The idiom "apple of my eye" conveys a deep sense of affection, value, and priority. Just as the eye is a vital and delicate organ that we instinctively protect, referring to a loved one as the "apple" of our eye emphasizes their importance and the depth of our care for them. The phrase evokes a sense of treasuring the most cherished, looking after the invaluable, and recognizing the profound bonds that tie us to those we love most. In using this idiom, speakers highlight the special place someone holds in their heart, placing them above all others in terms of love and esteem.

Cool as a Cucumber

The idiom "cool as a cucumber" describes someone who remains calm and composed, even in stressful or challenging situations. If someone is said to be as "cool as a cucumber," it means they are not easily flustered or disturbed.

Origin

1. Botanical Basis: Cucumbers have a reputation for being cool to the touch, especially when compared to the surrounding air. This is due to their high water content and the fact that they can retain moisture inside, keeping them cool even in hot conditions.

2. Literary References: The phrase can be traced back to early English literature. One of the earliest recorded uses was in John Gay's poem, "New Song on New Similes," written in 1732, where he states, "Cool as a cucumber could see the rest of womankind."

Example Sentence

"Even when the project deadline was moved up, Janet remained as cool as a cucumber and managed to get everything done on time."

The phrase "cool as a cucumber" paints a vivid picture of composure and unflappability. The cucumber, with its refreshing qualities, serves as an apt metaphor for a demeanor that remains undisturbed despite external pressures. In a world filled with stressors and challenges, being compared to this cool, calm vegetable is a compliment. It suggests resilience, steadiness, and the ability to think clearly even when faced with adversity. Using this idiom offers an illustrative way to praise someone's calm demeanor or to express one's own equanimity in the face of challenges.

Carrot and Stick

Meaning

The idiom "carrot and stick" refers to a motivational tactic that uses a combination of rewards (the carrot) and punishment (the stick) to encourage desired behavior. In other words, it's a method that simultaneously offers benefits for compliance and consequences for non-compliance.

Origin

1. Literal Imagery: The imagery conjured by the phrase stems from the act of dangling a carrot in front of a mule or donkey to entice it to move forward, while also holding a stick behind it as a threat of a prod or beat if it refuses to move. The animal is motivated to move towards the carrot (because it wants the reward) and away from the stick (because it wants to avoid the punishment).

2. Usage History: The exact origin is a bit muddy, with no clear first usage. However, the concept of combined reward and punishment has ancient roots and has been a fundamental aspect of human behavioral psychology.

Example Sentence

"To ensure the team meets its sales targets, the manager adopted a carrot and stick approach, offering bonuses for high performers and warnings to those who lagged behind."

The "carrot and stick" idiom encapsulates a fundamental aspect of human nature: we are motivated both by the allure of rewards and the aversion to unpleasant consequences. The phrase has been adopted in various fields, from business to education, to describe strategies that balance positive reinforcement with negative reinforcement. At its heart, "carrot and stick" speaks to the duality of motivation and the multifaceted ways in which individuals and groups can be encouraged to act or change behavior. However, it's worth noting that the effectiveness of such a tactic can vary, and relying too heavily on either the carrot or the stick might not yield desired results in every situation.

Have Your Cake and Eat It Too

The idiom "have your cake and eat it too" refers to wanting to enjoy two incompatible benefits or situations at the same time. It's often used to indicate a desire to have things both ways, typically in situations where it's not possible to retain a particular good or condition while also consuming or using it.

Origin

1. Historical Phrasing: The current phrasing seems somewhat illogical at first, because naturally, if you have a cake, you'd want to eat it. However, older forms of this saying make its meaning clearer. Earlier versions, such as "you can't eat your cake and have it too," highlight the inherent contradiction: once you eat your cake, you won't have it anymore.

2. Usage History: The expression has been used in English since the 16th century. The exact origins are not definitively traced, but the idiom has persisted for centuries, with its meaning remaining consistent even as the phrasing evolved.

Example Sentence

"She wants to live in the city to be close to her job but also yearns for the tranquility of the countryside. It's like she wants to have her cake and eat it too."

The idiom "have your cake and eat it too" encapsulates the human desire to possess and enjoy all benefits, even when they are inherently contradictory or mutually exclusive. It underscores the often unrealistic expectations people might have about outcomes or situations. In essence, the saying serves as a reminder of the need for compromise, for life often requires us to make choices where retaining all advantages is not possible. The allure of the saying, aside from its vivid imagery, lies in its universal applicability; everyone, at some point or another, grapples with wanting conflicting things and must reconcile with the realities of choice and consequence.

Chew the Fat

The idiom "chew the fat" means to chat or engage in casual conversation, often without any specific purpose or topic in mind. It suggests a relaxed and leisurely discussion, typically one that is friendly and informal.

Origin

1. Nautical Roots: One popular theory posits that the phrase has naval origins. Sailors during long sea voyages would chew on salt-hardened fat or salt pork when food supplies ran low. As this was a tough food to eat and took a while to chew, sailors would engage in conversations during the process, leading to the association of "chewing the fat" with casual talk.

2. Traditional Gatherings: Another theory suggests that in older times, people would gather and converse while chewing on animal fat, which was a common snack. The act of chewing and conversing blended into one, leading to the use of the idiom.

3. Oral Traditions: The act of "chewing" in various cultures and languages often has ties to discussions, mulling over ideas, or pondering, suggesting that the idiom could also be linked to the universal concept of oral traditions and conversation.

Example Sentence

"Every weekend, the neighbors gather on the porch to chew the fat and catch up on local news."

"Chew the fat" conjures up images of leisurely, unhurried conversations, emphasizing the casual and relaxed nature of such interactions. It taps into the universal human practice of bonding over shared moments, be it around food, a fire, or simply in each other's company. The phrase reminds us of the simple pleasures of human connection, the act of sharing stories, experiences, and ideas without any specific agenda or purpose other than to enjoy the act of communication itself. It's a celebration of camaraderie, community, and the age-old tradition of storytelling.

Eat Humble Pie

The idiom "eat humble pie" refers to the act of admitting one's mistakes or acknowledging one's wrongdoing, often with a feeling of humiliation or embarrassment. When someone says they had to "eat humble pie," they are conveying that they had to admit fault or apologize after previously being confident or arrogant about a particular matter.

Origin

1. Medieval Cuisine: The term "humble pie" derives from "umbles pie", which was a dish made from the offal (internal organs) of deer. "Umbles" referred to the less desirable parts of the animal, which were often eaten by the lower classes or servants in medieval England, while the more sought-after cuts went to the lords and nobles. Eating "umbles pie" was, therefore, associated with a lower status.

2. A Play on Words: Over time, the word "umbles" became phonetically confused with "humble", leading to the modern-day phrase. The connection between the dish made from the least desirable parts of the deer and the act of humility or lowering oneself is evident.

3. Literary Use: The phrase's use in literature and other written works over the centuries has solidified its meaning in the English language. It often appeared in contexts where characters or individuals had to come down from their high horses, admit faults, or show humility.

Example Sentence

"After boasting that he would easily win the race, John had to eat humble pie when he came in last."

"Eat humble pie" invokes imagery of humility and atonement. It paints a vivid picture of the often difficult act of admitting one's errors, especially after a display of overconfidence. This idiom captures the universal experience of facing the consequences of one's arrogance or miscalculations. At its core, "eat humble pie" serves as a reminder of the human tendency to overestimate oneself and the subsequent grounding experience of confronting reality. It highlights the importance of humility, the recognition of one's limitations, and the grace required to admit when one is wrong.

Full of Beans

Meaning

The idiom "full of beans" describes someone who is energetic, lively, and spirited. It can also mean someone who is full of enthusiasm and excitement. Occasionally, the phrase might be used to indicate someone who is not telling the truth or is misinformed, although this is a less common usage.

Origin

1. Livestock and Feed: The origin of the phrase is believed to be related to horses. In the past, beans were part of a horse's diet, especially for those horses that needed to be in high spirits and full of energy. Feeding beans to horses made them lively, leading to the association of beans with energy and liveliness.

2. Shift in Meaning: Over time, the term began to be applied to people, especially children or young individuals who exhibited high energy levels. The connotation of misinformation or "being full of it" is a more modern twist, where "beans" might be a euphemism for nonsense or falsehoods.

3. Popular Use: The phrase has been popularized in literature, films, and day-to-day conversations, especially in the context of describing youthful exuberance or playful energy.

Example Sentence

"The kids, full of beans after eating their candy, were running around the garden playing tag."

"Full of beans" conveys a sense of unbridled energy and joy, often reminiscent of the carefree days of childhood when one's spirit seems indefatigable. The idiom taps into the vivaciousness of life, the bursts of enthusiasm we experience, and the sheer zest of living. Whether it's the vision of a child playing without a care in the world or an adult taking on challenges with renewed vigor, "full of beans" encapsulates the essence of life's energetic moments. It serves as a reminder of the infectious energy that each of us can exhibit, impacting not just our own experiences but also those of the people around us.

Hot Potato

Meaning

The idiom "hot potato" refers to a controversial issue or situation that is awkward or unpleasant and that no one wants to handle or deal with. When someone describes a topic or matter as a "hot potato," they are emphasizing the sensitivity or contentiousness of the subject.

Origin

1. Physical Sensation: The origin of the phrase is quite literal. A hot potato is uncomfortable to hold for an extended period, and one's natural reaction is to quickly pass it to someone else or drop it. This physical sensation became a metaphor for tricky situations or subjects that people would rather not deal with or would like to pass on to someone else.

2. Games and Pastimes: Historically, there was a game called 'hot potato' where people would sit in a circle and toss a small object (like a beanbag) to each other while music played. The aim was to not be the last person holding the 'potato' when the music stopped. This game mirrors the idea of not wanting to be left handling an undesirable or tricky situation.

3. Modern Context: As the phrase evolved in modern English, it began to be applied more broadly to anything that was contentious, risky, or unpopular, especially in politics or social contexts.

Example Sentence

"The issue of tax reforms became a hot potato during the election, with no candidate wanting to commit to a firm stance."

"Hot potato" evokes imagery of urgency, discomfort, and evasion. It captures the human inclination to avoid confrontation or responsibility for difficult issues, and the desire to pass these challenges onto others. In a broader sense, the idiom speaks to societal or communal issues that might be universally acknowledged but rarely confronted directly due to their divisive or problematic nature. The term serves as a reminder that, while it's human nature to avoid difficult situations, truly addressing a "hot potato" often requires courage, directness, and a willingness to face discomfort head-on.

Bread and Butter

The idiom "bread and butter" generally has two primary meanings. Firstly, it can refer to a person's main source of income or livelihood – the primary means by which someone sustains themselves. Secondly, it can denote basic, essential, or staple elements of something, especially when referring to the main or most straightforward tasks of a job or activity.

Origin

1. Staple Foods: Historically, bread and butter have been fundamental components of many diets, particularly in Western cultures. Bread represents sustenance, while butter, which adds flavor, symbolizes a touch of luxury or added value. Together, they represent the basic necessities of life.

2. Economic Significance: In earlier times, having bread and butter signified a baseline of economic stability. If a person had bread and butter, it meant they were at least meeting their most basic needs, even if they couldn't afford more luxurious foods.

3. Broadening of Meaning: As societies evolved and jobs diversified, the term began to be applied metaphorically to describe any primary or fundamental source of income or the most basic tasks of a particular role or job. The phrase has been adopted in various industries and contexts to denote the core aspects of a given task or responsibility.

Example Sentence

1. *"For many writers, freelance articles are their bread and butter until they can publish a best-selling novel."*
2. *"Customer support is the bread and butter of our company. It's the primary service we offer, and the main reason clients trust us."*

The idiom "bread and butter" taps into the universal understanding of the need for sustenance and the basics that keep us going, whether in terms of food or income. It reminds us of the foundational elements upon which more complex or luxurious aspects of life can be built. In an era where aspirations and ambitions often reach for the stars, "bread and butter" serves as a grounding phrase, emphasizing the importance of ensuring that basic needs are met before branching out into more elaborate endeavors. Whether in a personal or professional context, it underscores the value of solidity, reliability, and the core elements that sustain us day-to-day.

Salt of the Earth

The idiom "salt of the earth" is used to describe a person or group of people who are considered to be of great worth, reliability, and fundamental goodness. Such individuals are often characterized by their straightforwardness, honesty, and humility. They're the kind of people who are dependable and unpretentious.

Origin

1. Biblical Roots: The phrase has its origins in the Bible. In the Sermon on the Mount, Jesus refers to his followers as the "salt of the earth" in the book of Matthew (5:13). In ancient times, salt was a highly valued commodity, used for preserving food and for its antiseptic qualities. Jesus' analogy implied that his followers, like salt, had a vital role in preserving the moral well-being of society.

2. Value of Salt: In ancient cultures, salt was not only an essential dietary item but was also used as a method of payment at times. The word "salary" is derived from the Latin word "salarium," which was a payment made to Roman soldiers for the purchase of salt. This emphasizes the significant value placed on salt in ancient times.

3. Cultural Adoption: Over time, the term transcended its religious origins and entered the secular vernacular. It began to be used more broadly to describe genuine and upright individuals, regardless of their religious affiliations.

Example Sentence

"Mister Thompson, who volunteers at the local shelter and helps maintain the town's gardens, is truly the salt of the earth."

The idiom "salt of the earth" evokes images of purity, preservation, and essential value. In using this phrase, one pays homage to those foundational members of society who, though they might not always be in the limelight, play a crucial role in maintaining the integrity and moral fabric of a community. Such individuals often work silently in the background, ensuring stability and offering unwavering support. They embody qualities of humility, hard work, and sincerity. The term reminds us of the immense value of character and authenticity in a world that often prioritizes flashiness and superficiality over depth and genuine goodness.

Salt in the Wound

Meaning

The idiom "salt in the wound" refers to making an already painful or difficult situation even worse, either unintentionally or deliberately. It suggests that someone is adding to the distress or discomfort of another person who is already upset, hurt, or facing difficulty.

Origin

1. Historical Context: Historically, salt was used as a disinfectant for wounds, especially in battlefield conditions. Although it might have had antiseptic properties, pouring salt on an open wound would cause significant pain to the injured person. This physical act serves as the foundation for the metaphorical use of the phrase.

2. Ancient Medicine: Salt's antiseptic properties were known in ancient times, and it was commonly used for preservation and disinfection. However, despite its benefits in preventing infection, the immediate consequence was intense stinging and pain.

3. Expansion of Meaning: Over time, the phrase moved from its literal interpretation to a metaphorical one, encapsulating any action or word that exacerbates an already negative or painful situation.

Example Sentence

"After losing the match, hearing the fans' criticism was like adding salt to the wound."

The idiom "salt in the wound" captures the essence of compounded pain or discomfort. It draws a vivid picture of an already difficult situation being made even more unbearable. The phrase serves as a reminder to be sensitive and compassionate, especially when dealing with someone who is already experiencing hardship or distress. In interactions and communications, it underscores the importance of timing and tact, emphasizing the potential harm of thoughtless remarks or actions in delicate situations.

A Taste of Your Own Medicine

The idiom "a taste of your own medicine" refers to experiencing the same treatment or circumstances that one has subjected others to, especially when this treatment is unpleasant or negative. It implies a kind of poetic justice where someone faces the same consequences or feelings that they have previously caused for someone else.

Origin

1. Biblical Roots: The concept of "an eye for an eye" or receiving equivalent treatment in return for one's actions has ancient roots and can be found in various cultures and religious texts, including the Bible.

2. Historical Usage: The exact phrase "a taste of your own medicine" seems to derive from the idea of doctors or healers being made to consume their own concoctions. If they were peddling ineffective or harmful treatments, they would directly experience the effects.

3. Figurative Expansion: Over time, the phrase began to be employed in a broader context, moving beyond literal medicine to any scenario where someone gets a dose of their own tactics or treatment.

Example Sentence

"After years of playing pranks on his coworkers, Jake finally got a taste of his own medicine when they surprised him with an elaborate hoax."

The idiom "a taste of your own medicine" captures the idea of poetic justice and retribution. It serves as a reminder that actions have consequences and that, at times, the universe has a way of ensuring that one experiences firsthand what they've made others go through. Whether employed in playful jest or to highlight genuine karmic retribution, the expression underscores the cyclical nature of actions and their repercussions. In societal and interpersonal contexts, it often functions as a call for empathy, suggesting that one might think twice about their actions if they consider how they'd feel being on the receiving end.

Breadwinner

Meaning

The idiom "breadwinner" refers to the primary or sole individual in a household or family who earns money to support the family. This person takes on the main financial responsibility for providing the basic needs such as food, shelter, and clothing.

Origin

1. Literal Interpretation: Historically, bread has been a staple food in many cultures. Earning one's daily bread or providing bread meant ensuring sustenance or livelihood. Therefore, the one who brought home the bread was essentially ensuring the survival and well-being of the family.

2. Evolution Over Time: The term "breadwinner" began to be used in English in the early 19th century, though the concept of a primary earner is much older. As societies evolved and the complexities of economies grew, the term began to encompass broader responsibilities beyond just ensuring daily food.

3. Societal Implications: Traditionally, in many cultures, the role of the breadwinner was primarily associated with men. However, as societies evolved and gender roles became more fluid, women also increasingly took on the role of breadwinners, challenging traditional norms and expectations.

Example Sentence

"With her husband laid off from work, Maria became the sole breadwinner for the family, working two jobs to ensure they had everything they needed."

The idiom "breadwinner" encapsulates the sense of duty, responsibility, and commitment that an individual feels towards the well-being and sustenance of their family or dependents. It speaks to the often challenging role of ensuring financial stability in a household and the sacrifices many make in this position. As economies and societies continue to change, the traditional image of the breadwinner has also evolved, reflecting shifts in economic realities, societal norms, and gender roles.

Egg on Your Face

Meaning

To have "egg on your face" means to be embarrassed or made to look foolish due to one's own actions, mistakes, or blunders. It refers to a situation where someone is caught in an awkward or compromising position, often in front of others.

Origin

1. Literal Interpretation: The visual image of someone having egg on their face is undeniably messy and awkward. While the precise origins of this idiom are unclear, the phrase likely draws from the comical and embarrassing sight of someone having food (in this case, egg) smeared on their face unintentionally.

2. Performance and Entertainment: One theory suggests that the phrase could have origins in slapstick comedy or vaudeville performances, where performers might literally end up with egg on their faces for comedic effect.

3. Evolution of Usage: Over time, the phrase transitioned from a possible literal context to a figurative one, capturing the essence of public embarrassment or being caught off-guard in a less than flattering situation.

Example Sentence

"After confidently asserting that he knew the answer during the meeting, and then realizing he was wrong, Jake felt like he had egg on his face."

The idiom "egg on your face" vividly encapsulates the feeling of embarrassment or humiliation, especially when one's own actions lead to that situation. It serves as a humorous way to describe those moments in life when things don't go as planned, and one is left feeling exposed or foolish. Whether it's making an incorrect statement with confidence or undertaking an action that backfires, having "egg on your face" is a relatable experience for many, reminding us of the human tendency to err and the importance of humility.

Wine and Dine

Meaning

To "wine and dine" someone means to entertain or treat them lavishly, often by taking them out to a fine dining restaurant, offering them good wine, and ensuring they have an enjoyable evening. It can be used in both personal and professional contexts, whether to impress, woo, or influence someone.

Origin

1. Historical Affluence: The act of entertaining guests with good food and wine has ancient roots, especially among the upper classes. Celebratory feasts, diplomatic dinners, and courtly banquets have long been a part of human culture.

2. Cultural Significance of Wine: Wine has historically been associated with sophistication and luxury. In many cultures, sharing wine was seen as a form of bonding and a sign of generosity.

3. Modern Context: As dining out became more commonplace in the 20th century, especially with the emergence of upscale restaurants, the practice of taking someone out for an elaborate meal, paired with fine wine, to impress or establish rapport became more widespread. The phrase "wine and dine" likely evolved as a catchy way to describe this act.

Example Sentence

"The company decided to wine and dine the potential investors, hoping to secure a significant deal by the end of the evening."

The idiom "wine and dine" touches on the cultural and social significance of food and drink as tools of persuasion, bonding, and celebration. It signifies the human penchant for using shared culinary experiences as a means to foster connections, build relationships, or make a lasting impression. In contemporary use, it often evokes images of sophistication, indulgence, and the idea that one is being treated to something special. Whether in the context of romantic pursuits, business dealings, or simple acts of generosity, "wine and dine" underscores the power of a memorable meal in shaping interactions and outcomes.

Travel and Movement

Hit the Road

The idiom "hit the road" is an informal way of saying to begin a journey or to depart from a place. It's often used to indicate that it's time to leave or move on.

Origin

1. Automobile Era: The phrase likely originated in the United States and became popular with the rise of automobile travel in the 20th century. As roads and highways became more widespread, they played a significant role in American culture and lexicon.

2. Physical Imagination: The term "hit" in this context could be imagined as the tires of a vehicle "hitting" or making contact with the road, symbolizing the commencement of a journey.

3. Popular Culture: The phrase has been popularized in music, films, and literature, further embedding it in the American vernacular. One of the more notable references is in the song "Hit the Road Jack" by Ray Charles.

Example Sentence

"We've spent enough time here; let's hit the road before it gets dark."

The idiom "hit the road" captures the spirit of movement, adventure, and transition. It's a call to action, urging one to get moving, whether that's in the context of a literal journey or a metaphorical one. The phrase evokes a sense of urgency and decisiveness, emphasizing the importance of taking the initiative and forging ahead. Whether one is setting out on a cross-country road trip, leaving a job, or simply saying goodbye after a brief visit, "hit the road" is a casual, spirited way to announce one's departure and embrace the journey ahead.

The Whole Nine Yards

Meaning

The idiom "the whole nine yards" means everything, the entire amount, or the full extent of something. When someone gives or does "the whole nine yards," they are giving or doing everything possible.

Origin

The exact origins of "the whole nine yards" are a bit murky, and several theories attempt to explain its provenance:

1. World War II Aircraft Machine Guns: One theory suggests that fighter planes in World War II were equipped with ammunition belts that were nine yards long. When a pilot used up all his ammunition shooting at an enemy, he gave them "the whole nine yards."

2. Concrete Trucks: Another theory posits that the standard cement mixer truck's capacity (at least during a specific period) was nine cubic yards, and when it delivered a full load, it delivered "the whole nine yards."

3. Cloth Measurement: Historically, fabric bolts or rolls of cloth, especially for making suits, might have been sold in lengths of nine yards. Giving someone "the whole nine yards" would mean providing them with enough fabric for a complete outfit.

4. Scottish Kilts: Another variation of the cloth theory is that it took nine yards of cloth to make a traditional Scottish kilt.

5. Trench Warfare: Some suggest the phrase came from World War I trench warfare, where trenches were often nine yards long.

6. Graveyards: Yet another theory is that the standard grave depth is six feet, but in some places, it was nine yards, hence giving "the whole nine yards" meant giving everything.

However, no theory has definitive proof, and the true origin remains elusive.

Example Sentence

"When preparing for the community event, Lisa didn't just bring snacks; she brought drinks, games, and music—the whole nine yards."

The idiom "the whole nine yards" evokes a sense of completeness and thoroughness. It speaks to the idea of not holding back and giving or doing one's utmost. Whether in the context of a task, telling a story, or delivering on a promise, invoking "the whole nine yards" underscores a commitment to being comprehensive and exhaustive in one's efforts. It's a testament to effort, dedication, and a refusal to cut corners.

Backseat Driver

The idiom "backseat driver" refers to someone who gives unsolicited advice or instructions, especially when they are not in control of a situation. Originally, it described a passenger in a vehicle who constantly gave driving advice or criticized the driver's skills, despite not being in the driver's seat themselves. In a broader context, it denotes anyone who offers guidance without being asked, often in matters they are not directly involved in.

Origin

The phrase stems from the early days of automobile usage:

1. Automobile Era: With the advent of automobiles in the late 19th and early 20th centuries, driving became a new skill that many were still learning. As such, passengers, particularly those seated in the back, might feel compelled to give advice or voice their concerns about the driver's decisions, leading to the term "backseat driver."

2. Safety and Control: Due to the novelty of cars and the lack of initial safety features, early passengers might have felt more vulnerable and hence more likely to comment on or criticize a driver's choices, even if their advice was unsolicited.

3. Spatial Reference: The term literally relates to someone positioned in the backseat of a car, highlighting the distance and separation between them and the actual control (driver's seat). This spatial relationship is then extrapolated to other scenarios where someone is giving advice from a position of non-control.

Example Sentence

"Even though I was leading the project, Jane kept offering unsolicited advice on how things should be done. She's such a backseat driver."

The idiom "backseat driver" captures the universal human experience of receiving unsolicited advice. It serves as a reminder that while guidance can be helpful, it's essential to know when to step back and let others take the lead. The phrase encourages trust in others' abilities and the wisdom of recognizing boundaries. It's a call for respect, trust, and the understanding that sometimes, it's better to be a silent observer than an unnecessary adviser.

Off the Beaten Path

Meaning

The idiom "off the beaten path" refers to something that is out of the way, not well-known, or unconventional. It often describes places that are secluded, less traveled, or hidden from the usual tourist spots. In a broader context, it can refer to ideas, methods, or things that are unconventional or not mainstream.

Origin

The phrase has its roots in old travel and exploration contexts:

1. Travel and Exploration: Historically, well-trodden paths or roads were created by the constant footfall of travelers, traders, and explorers. These paths were the common routes, known to be relatively safe and direct. To venture "off the beaten path" was to deviate from these known routes, risking the unknown.

2. Nature and Wilderness: In the context of wilderness and nature exploration, areas that were "off the beaten path" were untouched, pristine, and often more challenging to navigate, further adding to the allure of discovery and adventure.

3. Cultural Evolution: As travel evolved and certain places became tourist hubs, the desire to find unique, unspoiled places led to the idiom's modern connotation – seeking experiences not typically found in guidebooks.

Example Sentence

"While most tourists visit the main attractions, we wanted to go off the beaten path and explore some lesser-known spots in the countryside."

The idiom "off the beaten path" encapsulates the spirit of adventure and discovery. It speaks to the desire to break away from the conventional and the known, to seek out experiences that are unique and untouched. Whether in the context of travel, thought, or action, the phrase challenges the norm and encourages the exploration of the unfamiliar. It's a call to embrace the unknown, to discover hidden gems, and to cherish experiences that are authentic and rare.

Hit the Ground Running

Meaning

The idiom "hit the ground running" describes the action of beginning a task or job with great enthusiasm, energy, and competence, without needing a gradual buildup or a period of adjustment. Essentially, it suggests immediately being effective or successful in a new endeavor or environment.

Origin

1. Military Origins: Some theories suggest that the idiom has roots in military paratrooper actions. When paratroopers jump from planes and land, they're trained to get up and move quickly, not wasting any time. In this context, to "hit the ground running" would mean to spring into action immediately upon landing.

2. Cattle Drives: Another theory relates to cattle drives in the U.S. When cattle were transported by train, they would often start running as soon as they were let out of the cattle cars, effectively "hitting the ground running."

3. Modern Business World: In the modern context, it has been popularized by the business world, referring to employees who start a new job or project and immediately show effectiveness without needing an extended period of training or orientation.

Example Sentence

"When she took over the management of the project, she really hit the ground running, making significant improvements in the first week."

The idiom "hit the ground running" conveys a sense of immediate action and effectiveness. It's a quality that's often sought after in the fast-paced environments of today, where there's a premium on being able to adapt and perform efficiently from the get-go. It's not just about speed, but also about competence and readiness, indicating that the individual or group is well-prepared, adaptable, and proactive. In a broader context, it underscores the value of preparedness and the ability to adapt swiftly to new challenges or environments.

Take a Rain Check

Meaning

The idiom "take a rain check" is used when someone cannot accept an invitation or offer at the current time but would like to take advantage of it later. It's a polite way of saying "I can't right now, but I'd like to in the future."

Origin

1. Baseball Origins: The phrase originated in the world of American baseball in the 19th century. If a baseball game was postponed due to rain, ticket holders were given a "rain check," which was essentially a replacement ticket for a rescheduled game or a future game.

2. Evolving Use: Over time, this concept of a replacement ticket extended to other areas, such as retail, where stores would offer a rain check to customers if a particular sale item was out of stock. The customer could return later to purchase the item at the sale price once it was back in stock.

3. Modern Figurative Use: The term has since evolved to its current colloquial use, indicating a desire or intention to take someone up on an offer or invitation at a later date, not just in specific situations like baseball or shopping.

Example Sentence

"I appreciate the invite to dinner tonight, but I'm swamped with work. Can I take a rain check and join you next week?"

The idiom "take a rain check" embodies the understanding and flexibility inherent in social and professional interactions. While originally grounded in the very specific world of baseball, its evolution to a broader, figurative meaning showcases the dynamic nature of language. In the hustle and bustle of modern life, where schedules can be unpredictable and commitments numerous, this phrase serves as a gentle reminder that while timing might not always align, the intention to connect and engage remains. It's a testament to the value of relationships and the mutual understanding that sometimes, things need to be postponed, but not forgotten.

Hitch Your Wagon to a Star

The idiom "hitch your wagon to a star" advises individuals to set high goals or to aim for ambitious achievements. It suggests aspiring to greatness or aligning oneself with something impressive or promising.

Origin

1. Ralph Waldo Emerson: The phrase is often attributed to the American essayist and poet Ralph Waldo Emerson. In his essay on "Civilization," he wrote: "Now that is the wisdom of a man, in every instance of his labor, to hitch his wagon to a star, and see his chore done by the gods themselves."

2. Astronomical Imagery: Stars have long been symbols of guidance, aspiration, and the infinite possibilities of the universe. The act of hitching one's wagon to such an entity signifies a grand ambition. The star serves as a beacon or guide, and the wagon, a symbol of one's efforts or endeavors, suggests that by connecting one's pursuits to a lofty goal, the journey, though challenging, will be directed towards greatness.

3. Cultural Evolution: Over time, the phrase has been adopted into popular culture and is used to describe the act of aiming high or attaching oneself to a promising venture or individual.

Example Sentence

"Rather than settling for mediocre results, she decided to hitch her wagon to a star and pursue her dream of becoming a renowned author."

The idiom "hitch your wagon to a star" speaks to the human spirit of ambition and the pursuit of excellence. It's a poetic way of emphasizing the importance of dreaming big and setting one's sights on lofty goals. Whether in personal or professional endeavors, this phrase serves as an inspiration, reminding individuals that by aiming for the stars, even if one falls short, they'll still be reaching great heights. In a world where it's easy to become complacent or settle for the status quo, "hitch your wagon to a star" is a motivational call to rise above the ordinary and aspire to the extraordinary.

Paddle Your Own Canoe

The idiom "paddle your own canoe" advises individuals to be self-reliant and independent, to take charge of their own destiny, and to make decisions for themselves without relying excessively on others.

Origin

1. Literal Interpretation: Canoeing requires skill, balance, and determination, especially if you're doing it alone. If one is paddling their own canoe, it means they are navigating and propelling themselves forward without the aid of others, representing independence and self-sufficiency.

2. Cultural and Literary References: The phrase was popularized in the 19th century, particularly in North America. In 1852, Sarah Tittle Bolton wrote a poem titled "Paddle Your Own Canoe," which had verses emphasizing the virtues of self-reliance and determination. This poetic work helped embed the idiom into popular culture.

3. Reflection of Individualism: The phrase is particularly resonant in cultures that place a strong emphasis on individualism and the pioneer spirit. The image of a lone canoeist navigating the waters can be seen as a metaphor for the individual navigating the challenges of life.

Example Sentence

"While it's good to listen to advice from others, it's important to ultimately paddle your own canoe and make decisions that are right for you."

The idiom "paddle your own canoe" is a timeless piece of advice that emphasizes the virtues of autonomy and personal responsibility. It suggests that while external assistance and guidance can be valuable, one must also be prepared to take initiative and steer their own course. In an ever-connected world, where opinions and suggestions can be easily sought, this phrase reminds individuals of the importance of self-agency, confidence in one's convictions, and the rewards of personal endeavor. Whether navigating the challenges of a personal project, a career move, or life's many decisions, "paddle your own canoe" serves as a nudge towards self-trust and initiative.

In the Same Boat

The idiom "in the same boat" describes a situation where two or more individuals are facing the same challenges or are in the same difficult circumstances. When people say they are "in the same boat," they are emphasizing shared experiences, problems, or challenges.

Origin

1. Nautical Beginnings: The phrase likely has its roots in the nautical world. Historically, being on a boat, especially during adverse conditions, required crew members to work together and cooperate. If the boat faced danger, everyone on it shared the same risk, regardless of their status or position.

2. Shared Responsibility and Outcome: The idea behind this idiom is that people on a boat have a mutual interest in working together to ensure the boat stays afloat. Their fates are intertwined, much like individuals facing the same challenge or adversity in other contexts.

3. Cultural Integration: Over time, the phrase was adopted into everyday language and was used to refer to any shared situation, not just nautical ones. It captures the human experience of camaraderie, shared fate, and collective challenge.

Example Sentence

"Due to the economic downturn, many companies are facing financial difficulties. We're all in the same boat, trying to find ways to stay afloat."

The phrase "in the same boat" encapsulates a universal truth about shared human experience. At various times in life, individuals find themselves facing challenges that are also being faced by others. Recognizing this shared struggle can foster empathy, solidarity, and collaboration. In a world with diverse experiences and backgrounds, this idiom serves as a reminder of the commonalities people often share. Whether facing global crises, community challenges, or personal hurdles, the idea of being "in the same boat" underscores the importance of unity, mutual support, and collective action.

Keep Your Nose to the Grindstone

Meaning

The idiom "keep your nose to the grindstone" advises someone to continue working hard and stay focused on the task at hand. It's often used to emphasize dedication, persistence, and effort in one's work or duties.

Origin

1. Literal Interpretation: Historically, a grindstone is a flat, round stone used for sharpening tools or grinding grain. When sharpening blades, a craftsman would need to hold the blade against the grindstone at a precise angle, requiring sustained attention and effort. Hence, "keeping one's nose to the grindstone" would mean focusing on the work and not getting distracted.

2. Evolution of the Phrase: There's some debate over whether the phrase originally referred to the continuous labor of using a grindstone or to the posture adopted by someone using it. Regardless, over time, it became a metaphor for dedication and hard work.

3. Variations: An earlier related phrase, "to hold one's nose to the grindstone," was recorded in the early 16th century. The current version, with "keep," became more popular and is the one predominantly used today.

Example Sentence

"If you want to finish this project before the deadline, you'll need to keep your nose to the grindstone."

The idiom "keep your nose to the grindstone" is a testament to the virtues of hard work, dedication, and perseverance. In various spheres of life, be it professional, academic, or personal, sustained effort often becomes crucial for achieving success. This phrase resonates with the idea that success doesn't come easy and that one must remain committed and focused to see a task through. It acts as a motivational reminder that diligence pays off and distractions must be set aside to accomplish one's goals.

Road Less Traveled

Meaning

The idiom "road less traveled" refers to a path or approach that is not commonly chosen or a route that is unconventional. In a broader sense, it can be used to describe a decision, lifestyle, or course of action that is different from what is typical or expected. It often carries with it a connotation of bravery or individualism in choosing a unique path.

Origin

1. Literary Roots: The phrase "road less traveled" finds its roots in the poem "The Road Not Taken" by Robert Frost, published in 1916. In the poem, the narrator stands at a crossroads in a forest and must decide which of two roads to take. He chooses the one "less traveled by," symbolizing the choices we make in life. The poem, and especially its ending lines, have since been widely quoted and referenced.

2. Interpretative Layers: Frost's poem is often interpreted as a celebration of individualism and forging one's own path. However, deeper readings suggest it might be more about the nature of choices and the inevitable regret of paths not taken.

3. Popularization: Over time, the phrase has been adopted and adapted into popular culture, sometimes even deviating from its original introspective tone to imply an adventurous or unconventional choice.

Example Sentence

"Instead of following the traditional route in his career, he decided to take the road less traveled and started his own business."

The idiom "road less traveled" evokes a spirit of individualism and the courage to choose paths that might be fraught with challenges but also potential rewards. In a world where conformity often seems easier, the phrase celebrates those who dare to be different, to think outside the box, and to carve out their own niche. Whether it's in personal choices, professional pursuits, or philosophical beliefs, taking the "road less traveled" implies a certain boldness in defying the norm. It's a reminder that sometimes, the most fulfilling journeys are those that aren't commonly taken.

Miles Away

Meaning

The idiom "miles away" doesn't usually refer to physical distance. Instead, it's used to describe someone who is lost in thought or daydreaming, not paying attention to the present moment. When someone says you seem "miles away," they mean you seem distracted or not mentally present.

Origin

1. Literal Meaning: Originally, the term would have been used to describe actual physical distance. Saying something or someone was "miles away" would have meant just that—they were a considerable distance away.

2. Figurative Shift: Over time, like many idioms, the phrase began to be used in a more figurative sense. This is common in the English language, where physical distances or locations are used to describe mental or emotional states, such as "being in another world" or "head in the clouds."

3. Expansion of Use: As the idiom's usage expanded, it came to symbolize not just physical distance, but emotional or mental distance. This shift reflects the human tendency to describe internal experiences in terms of external physical spaces.

Example Sentence

"I asked her twice if she wanted coffee, but she was miles away and didn't hear me."

The phrase "miles away" encapsulates the idea that our minds can travel far from our current situation, even if our bodies remain in one place. It's a testament to the power of the human mind to wander, to daydream, and to become deeply engrossed in thought. Whether reminiscing about the past, pondering the future, or simply drifting into a daydream, being "miles away" is a universal experience that underscores the depth and richness of our inner worlds.

Jump on the Bandwagon

The idiom "jump on the bandwagon" refers to joining a popular activity, cause, or movement, especially one that has gained widespread acceptance or popularity. It often carries a somewhat negative connotation, suggesting that the person is following a trend without deeply considering or believing in it, but simply because many others are doing so.

Origin

1. Political Roots: The term "bandwagon" originally referred to a wagon used to carry a circus band. During the mid-19th century in the United States, politicians would use bandwagons during parades to generate excitement and attract attention.

2. Use in Campaigns: As some politicians gained popularity, more people would literally jump onto their bandwagon, wanting to be associated with a potential winner. P.T. Barnum, the famous showman, is credited with adding to this phenomenon by parading his bandwagon through towns to drum up interest for his circus, leading others to literally and figuratively "jump on" when something became popular.

3. Figurative Meaning: Over time, the phrase evolved to have a more figurative meaning, suggesting that people were joining a cause not necessarily because they believed in it, but because it was popular and they wanted to be associated with a winning or popular side.

Example Sentence

"As soon as the team started winning, everyone wanted to jump on the bandwagon and show their support."

The phrase "jump on the bandwagon" encapsulates the human tendency to gravitate towards what is currently popular or successful, often without genuine passion or understanding. It highlights the idea that people often want to be part of something bigger, especially if it's seen as the "winning" side, even if their commitment might be shallow or temporary. The idiom serves as a cautionary note, reminding individuals to be genuine in their pursuits and not merely follow the crowd.

Go the Extra Mile

The idiom "go the extra mile" refers to making more effort than is required or expected. It suggests doing more than what is necessary, typically to assist someone, achieve a goal, or make a positive impression.

Origin

1. Biblical Origins: This phrase has its roots in the New Testament of the Bible. In the Sermon on the Mount, Jesus is quoted in the Gospel of Matthew (5:41) as saying, "And whosoever shall compel thee to go a mile, go with him twain." In ancient Roman times, a Roman soldier could legally compel a Jewish civilian to carry his equipment for one Roman mile, which is about 1,000 paces (roughly 4,800 feet, somewhat shorter than the modern mile). Jesus's teaching suggested that if asked to go one mile, one should willingly go two, emphasizing generosity and self-sacrifice.

2. Expansion in Usage: Over time, the religious undertones of the phrase became less prominent, and it began to be used more broadly to mean putting in extra effort or doing more than is required in any situation, not just in the context of a compelled service.

Example Sentence

"To ensure the project was a success, Maria was always willing to go the extra mile, working late and helping her colleagues."

"Go the extra mile" speaks to the value of hard work, dedication, and a willingness to exceed expectations. It celebrates the spirit of giving more than is asked and emphasizes the potential rewards of such diligence and commitment. The idiom serves as an inspiration and reminder that, often, success and appreciation come to those who consistently offer more than the minimum required effort.

On the Right Track

The idiom "on the right track" refers to being correctly oriented or following the correct path or approach towards a particular goal or solution. It suggests that progress is being made in a desirable direction.

Origin

1. Railroad Imagery: The word "track" in the phrase likely derives from the tracks that trains run on. When a train is on the right track, it moves smoothly toward its destination without hindrance. Conversely, being on the "wrong track" would mean that the train is headed in the wrong direction or toward potential danger.

2. Guidance and Navigation: Historically, before the advent of modern navigation tools, travelers and explorers relied on landmarks and other natural indicators to ensure they were on the correct path. Being "on the right track" would mean they were correctly oriented towards their intended destination.

3. Analytical Problem Solving: In more abstract contexts, such as problem-solving or investigations, the idiom might have been used to indicate that one's line of thinking or approach was correct and would likely lead to the solution.

Example Sentence

"After weeks of struggling with the research, when Jane found the old manuscript, she felt she was finally on the right track."

The idiom "on the right track" reflects a sense of affirmation and optimism. It is often used to convey confidence in one's choices or to reassure someone that their efforts are leading them in a positive direction. Whether used in the context of physical journeys, intellectual pursuits, or personal growth, the phrase embodies the importance of perseverance, direction, and alignment with one's goals.

By the Skin of Your Teeth

The idiom "by the skin of your teeth" means to narrowly escape from a situation or to achieve something by a very small margin. When someone says they did something "by the skin of their teeth," they are emphasizing how close they were to failing or facing a negative outcome.

Origin

1. Biblical Reference: This phrase has ancient origins and is found in the Book of Job in the Old Testament of the Bible. In Job 19:20, Job, who faced numerous hardships and afflictions, says, "My bone cleaveth to my skin and to my flesh, and I am escaped with the skin of my teeth." Given that teeth don't have skin, the expression is a hyperbolic way to describe a very narrow escape.

2. Evolution of Usage: Over the centuries, the phrase has been adopted and adapted into common English vernacular. Its figurative meaning, emphasizing the thinness or non-existence of "skin" on teeth, underscores just how narrow an escape or margin is being referred to.

3. Cultural Transmission: The widespread influence of the Bible in English-speaking societies meant that many of its phrases became integrated into everyday language. "By the skin of your teeth" is one of these phrases that transitioned from a religious text to common parlance.

Example Sentence

"He managed to pass the exam by the skin of his teeth, getting the exact score needed to pass."

The idiom "by the skin of your teeth" captures the essence of close calls and narrow escapes. It is a vivid way to describe situations where there's little to no room for error, and it underscores the relief and sometimes surprise that comes with such outcomes. Whether it's in sports, academics, or everyday life challenges, the phrase highlights the thin line between success and failure.

Fly by the Seat of One's Pants

The idiom "fly by the seat of one's pants" refers to relying on instinct and intuition rather than careful planning or formal methodology. It means to improvise or make decisions based on the current situation, often in the absence of experience or adequate information.

Origin

1. Aviation Origins: The phrase originates from the early days of aviation. Airplanes lacked sophisticated instruments, and pilots had to rely heavily on their physical senses and perceptions when flying. The "seat of the pants" refers to a pilot's feeling of the aircraft's movements through the seat, allowing them to gauge the aircraft's behavior in the absence of visual references or reliable instruments.

2. Sensory Flight: Without advanced instrumentation, early pilots often had to rely on how the aircraft's vibrations and movements felt against their body, especially during poor visibility conditions, to make flight decisions.

3. From Cockpit to Common Use: Over time, the term was adopted more broadly to describe any situation where someone proceeds or makes decisions based on instinct, immediate perceptions, or incomplete information, rather than following a structured plan or relying on extensive knowledge.

Example Sentence

"Without any formal training in event management, Jenna had to fly by the seat of her pants to organize the company's annual gala."

The idiom "fly by the seat of one's pants" encapsulates the idea that sometimes, in the absence of concrete data or a clear path, one must rely on gut feelings, intuition, and immediate perceptions to navigate a situation. It speaks to the human ability to adapt, improvise, and make the best of uncertain circumstances. While it can sometimes denote recklessness or lack of preparation, it also celebrates the spirit of resourcefulness and the capacity to think on one's feet in challenging scenarios. In an ever-changing world, the ability to "fly by the seat of one's pants" is often an invaluable skill, whether in the cockpit of a plane or the complexities of daily life.

Sail Close to the Wind

Meaning

The idiom "sail close to the wind" refers to someone who is taking risks by behaving in a way that might have negative consequences or get them into trouble. It can also refer to someone operating at the borderline of what is considered acceptable or legal.

Origin

1. Nautical Roots: The phrase has its roots in sailing. When a ship sails close to the wind, it is sailing as nearly as possible in the direction from which the wind is coming, a maneuver that requires skill and can be risky. Sailing too close to the wind can cause the sails to lose their wind, making the ship stall or lose speed.

2. Navigational Challenge: Sailors of old would sometimes sail close to the wind when trying to make as much headway as possible in an upwind direction. It was a tactic used to get to a destination faster but required careful balancing. If done incorrectly, it could lead to a loss of control over the vessel.

3. Metaphorical Evolution: Over time, the phrase moved beyond its nautical context. It began to symbolize any action that bordered on danger, illegality, or impropriety, not just the specific sailing maneuver.

Example Sentence

"While his methods are effective, many believe he sails too close to the wind and might one day face serious consequences for his actions."

The idiom "sail close to the wind" emphasizes the delicate balance between taking risks to achieve one's goals and the potential hazards of such daring actions. In life, as in sailing, knowing how close one can get to potential danger without crossing into perilous territory is a valuable skill. This phrase serves as a reminder that while risk can lead to reward, it also comes with its own set of challenges and consequences. It encourages a careful evaluation of actions and decisions, especially when treading in or near controversial or hazardous zones.

Put the Cart Before the Horse

Meaning

The idiom "put the cart before the horse" describes a situation where things are done in the wrong order or sequence. It suggests that someone has reversed the natural or logical order of steps or priorities, leading to potential inefficiencies or problems.

Origin

1. Literal Imagery: Historically, carts were drawn by horses. The horse, providing the power and direction, logically comes before the cart it pulls. If one were to put the cart in front of the horse, it would not function properly, making the setup impractical and absurd.

2. Historical Usage: This phrase has been used in English since at least the 16th century. The idea, however, of doing things in the wrong order is much older and has been expressed in various ways in different languages and cultures throughout history.

3. Symbolism of Sequence: The imagery effectively conveys the importance of process and sequence in any endeavor. Just as a cart cannot push a horse, certain processes or tasks cannot (or should not) be undertaken until preceding steps have been completed.

Example Sentence

"Trying to design the cover of the book before its content is even written is like putting the cart before the horse."

The idiom "put the cart before the horse" serves as a cautionary phrase, reminding individuals of the importance of sequence, process, and timing. In our haste to achieve results or out of eagerness, we sometimes overlook foundational steps or priorities. This phrase is a nudge to reflect on whether we are approaching tasks and challenges in the right order. Whether in business, personal projects, or daily tasks, ensuring that the "horse" always precedes the "cart" can prevent unnecessary complications and pave the way for smoother progress.

Down to the Wire

The idiom "down to the wire" refers to a situation where the outcome is not decided until the very last moment or until the final opportunity. It suggests that results are uncertain and could go either way until the very end.

Origin

1. Horse Racing: The phrase originates from horse racing. In the past, a small wire was strung above the finish line to help judges determine which horse crossed the line first, especially during close races. If a race was "down to the wire," it meant that the outcome was undecided until the horses reached that finishing wire.

2. Symbolism of the Wire: The wire in horse racing served as a definitive marker, drawing a clear line between success and failure. As races became more competitive and results harder to predict, the tension and excitement of waiting for that last moment, the crossing of the wire, became symbolic of any close contest or situation.

3. Expansion Beyond Racing: Over time, the phrase moved beyond the world of horse racing and found its way into everyday language. It began to be applied to any scenario where results or outcomes were in doubt until the last possible moment, be it in sports, business, or personal situations.

Example Sentence

"The election was so close that it came down to the wire, with the final votes determining the winner."

The idiom "down to the wire" encapsulates the suspense and uncertainty inherent in close contests or situations. It speaks to the unpredictability of outcomes and the thrill of last-minute results. Whether used in the context of sports, negotiations, or daily challenges, the phrase emphasizes that, sometimes, things aren't decided until the very end, and perseverance is crucial. It also serves as a reminder that every moment counts, and it's essential to give one's best until the very last second.

Sports & Games

Jump the Gun

The idiom "jump the gun" means to act prematurely or to do something before it's the appropriate time. It suggests that someone is being hasty or impulsive, not waiting for the right moment or signal to act.

Origin

1. Track and Field: The phrase is believed to have originated from track and field races. In such races, a starter gun is fired to signal the beginning of the race. If a runner starts before the gun goes off, they have begun too early, hence "jumping the gun."

2. Usage in Sports Commentary: The phrase was popularized in the 20th century, especially in the context of sports commentary. As broadcasting of athletic events became more common, commentators would use "jump the gun" to describe false starts in races. This widespread use helped embed the idiom into everyday language.

3. Expansion into General Language: Over time, the term was adopted beyond sports to describe any situation where someone acted too soon or without the necessary preparation, further cementing its figurative meaning in everyday conversation.

Example Sentence

"He was so excited about the project that he jumped the gun and started working on it before getting the manager's approval."

"Jump the gun" conveys the idea that in our eagerness or impatience, we sometimes act without fully considering the right timing or the potential consequences. Whether in the context of work, relationships, or personal decisions, the idiom serves as a cautionary reminder of the importance of patience, preparation, and waiting for the right moment to act.

Ball Is in Your Court

Meaning

The idiom "the ball is in your court" means that it's now someone's turn to take action or respond to a situation. It signifies that the responsibility for the next step or move lies with that person. Essentially, the phrase is used to convey that it's up to them to decide or make the next move.

Origin

1. Tennis Origins: The phrase likely originates from the game of tennis. In tennis, players hit a ball back and forth over a net. When the ball is hit to one side, it becomes the responsibility of the player on that side to hit it back. Hence, if the "ball is in your court," it's your turn to play or respond.

2. Usage Beyond Sports: While the origin is tied to a sport, the phrase has been adopted more broadly to refer to any situation where responsibility or the need to take action has shifted to another person.

3. Reflection of Accountability: As the idiom became more integrated into everyday language, it began to reflect not just the concept of taking a turn, but also the idea of taking responsibility. When someone says "the ball is in your court," they're often emphasizing that it's now your duty to respond or act on a matter.

Example Sentence

"After I submitted my job application, the recruiter said they'd review it and get back to me. Now the ball is in their court."

The idiom "the ball is in your court" captures the essence of responsibility and agency. In the diverse game of life, decisions and actions constantly shift between individuals. Whether it's in a business negotiation, a personal relationship, or a decision-making process, this phrase reminds individuals of their active role and the significance of their choices. It serves to empower and also to hold individuals accountable for the next steps in any given situation.

Hitting Below the Belt

The idiom "hitting below the belt" refers to an action or remark that is considered unfair, unkind, or inappropriate. It signifies behavior that is deemed unacceptable or outside the bounds of fairness or decorum. In essence, it points to a breach of accepted standards or rules.

Origin

1. Boxing Origins: The phrase originates from the sport of boxing. In boxing, it's a foul to hit an opponent below the belt, referring to the waistline of the boxer's shorts, as it is considered a cheap and dangerous move.

2. Transition from Sport to Everyday Language: The term made its way from the boxing ring into everyday language to describe any form of deceitful, unfair, or underhanded action. Just as a low blow in boxing is against the rules and can cause undue harm, an action or comment "below the belt" in everyday scenarios signifies a breach of expected conduct.

3. Cultural Expansion of the Term: As the term became more ingrained in everyday vernacular, it started to encompass not just actions but also words or comments that were unnecessarily hurtful, unkind, or malicious.

Example Sentence

"When Mike brought up Sarah's personal problems during the debate, many felt he was hitting below the belt."

The idiom "hitting below the belt" serves as a reminder of the importance of fairness and integrity in interactions. It underscores the significance of ethical conduct and the unwritten rules that govern behavior, both in formal situations like sports or business and in personal relationships. The phrase also highlights the human tendency to sometimes act out of malice or desperation and the societal expectation to act within the bounds of decency.

Ace in the Hole

The idiom "ace in the hole" refers to a secret advantage or a hidden resource that one can use when the situation demands it. It signifies having a backup plan or a concealed strength that can be utilized to secure victory or success, especially in challenging circumstances.

Origin

1. Poker Origins: The phrase is believed to originate from the game of poker. In stud poker, players are dealt some cards face up and others face down. The cards that are face down, and therefore hidden from opponents, are called "hole" cards. Having an "ace in the hole" would mean possessing an ace card that is faced down, giving the player a secret and potentially game-winning advantage.

2. Transition to Broader Use: The term naturally transitioned from the poker table to general usage, symbolizing any secret advantage or resource that can be leveraged when needed. The ace, being the highest card in many card games, emphasizes the strength or value of this hidden resource.

3. Usage in Pop Culture and Literature: Over time, the phrase has been used in various forms of literature, movies, and songs, further ingraining its significance in popular culture. Its evocative imagery of a hidden trump card has made it a favorite among writers and speakers.

Example Sentence

"Everyone thought Anna would lose the negotiation, but she had an ace in the hole: she knew about the competitor's shortcomings."

The idiom "ace in the hole" highlights the strategy often employed in life's challenges – keeping certain advantages concealed until the opportune moment. It emphasizes the element of surprise in strategic decisions and the value of possessing undisclosed strengths or resources. In various situations, from business dealings to personal challenges, having an "ace in the hole" can be the difference between success and failure.

Knock it out of the Park

The idiom "knock it out of the park" refers to doing something exceptionally well or exceeding expectations in a particular task or venture. It can be used to describe a variety of achievements, not just those related to sports. When someone "knocks it out of the park," they have gone above and beyond, delivering results that impress or astonish.

Origin

1. Baseball Roots: This phrase finds its origins in the game of baseball. In baseball, if a player hits the ball hard enough for it to leave the field (i.e., go over the fence), it's considered a home run, which is one of the best outcomes for a batter. Hitting a ball out of the park means the batter has not only scored a run for their team but has also showcased exceptional skill.

2. Celebration of Excellence: Such a feat in baseball is often celebrated with great enthusiasm, both by the team and the fans. The impressive nature of this act, and the immediate, tangible result (the score), made "knocking it out of the park" synonymous with achieving great success.

3. Expansion Beyond Baseball: Over time, this phrase was adopted into general colloquial speech and began to be used in contexts outside of baseball. It became a metaphor for excelling in any endeavor, whether it's delivering a fantastic work presentation, achieving a personal goal, or impressing in a performance.

Example Sentence

"When Sarah presented her project proposal to the board, she really knocked it out of the park; everyone was impressed."

The idiom "knock it out of the park" celebrates moments of triumph and excellence, drawing from the visceral excitement of witnessing a baseball soaring over a fence. In broader contexts, it underscores the idea that with talent, dedication, and perhaps a touch of flair, one can deliver results that not only meet but also surpass expectations. It's an ode to those moments when individuals rise to the occasion and truly shine.

Play Hardball

The idiom "play hardball" refers to adopting a tough, uncompromising stance or approach in a situation, especially during negotiations or confrontations. Someone who "plays hardball" is not willing to easily compromise and often employs aggressive tactics to achieve their objectives.

Origin

1. Baseball Origins: The term "hardball" refers to the solid ball used in baseball, as opposed to the softer ball used in softball. Playing with a hardball can be considered more challenging and demanding, given the speed and impact with which it's thrown and hit.

2. Comparative Nature: The difference between baseball and softball and the inherent challenges of playing with a harder ball likely contributed to the figurative usage of the phrase. Over time, "playing hardball" began to symbolize an approach that was more aggressive and less yielding than a more "softball" or gentler approach.

3. Adoption in Business and Politics: As baseball terminology permeated American culture, "play hardball" was co-opted into the world of business and politics. Here, it came to represent a no-nonsense, assertive strategy, particularly during negotiations or when handling opposition.

Example Sentence

"When it came to the business merger, the company decided to play hardball and gave the competitors an ultimatum."

The idiom "play hardball" underscores the strategy and tactics that individuals or entities might use when stakes are high or when they believe a firm stance is required. While it can denote assertiveness and determination, it's also worth noting that "playing hardball" can sometimes be seen as overly aggressive or unyielding, which might not always be the best approach depending on the situation. As with many strategies, understanding when to "play hardball" and when to adopt a more conciliatory approach is key to successful outcomes.

Move the Goalposts

Meaning

The idiom "move the goalposts" means to change the criteria or standards during a process, usually making a task or objective more difficult to achieve. When someone is accused of "moving the goalposts," it typically implies an unfair or shifting standard that can be frustrating or disadvantageous to others.

Origin

1. Sporting Origins: The phrase likely originates from field games, such as football or rugby, where actual goalposts are used. If one were to imagine literally moving these goalposts during a game, it would change the conditions under which teams are playing, making it either easier or harder to score based on the new position.

2. Figurative Application: Given the clear unfairness that would result from literally moving goalposts during a sporting event, the phrase was adopted into colloquial language to represent any situation where the standards or rules are changed, usually to the disadvantage of one party.

3. Widespread Use: Over time, the idiom has been adopted in various fields like business, politics, and academia to describe situations where changing standards or expectations can create challenges or perceived injustices.

Example Sentence

"Jane was close to completing her project under the initial requirements, but her manager moved the goalposts and added more tasks."

The phrase "move the goalposts" serves as a reminder of the importance of consistency, fairness, and clear communication, especially when setting and pursuing objectives. The idiom reflects the frustration that can arise when expectations are changed without clear rationale or when the rules of engagement are perceived as being altered unfairly. In professional or personal endeavors, ensuring that the "goalposts" remain consistent can be crucial for motivation, trust, and successful outcomes.

Call the Shots

The idiom "call the shots" means to be in charge or to make the key decisions in a particular situation or endeavor. Someone who "calls the shots" is the one who controls what happens and dictates the terms or direction.

Origin

1. Sporting Origins: The expression likely has its roots in target shooting. In such contexts, a spotter or a marksman would "call" their shot by announcing where they intended to hit the target before taking their shot. Successfully hitting the called spot demonstrated skill and control.

2. Billiards Influence: Another theory ties the idiom to the game of billiards or pool. In some versions of these games, players are required to "call" or announce the pocket they intend to send a particular ball into. Successfully pocketing the ball in the declared pocket would mean the player accurately "called the shot."

3. Adoption in Broader Contexts: Over time, the phrase transcended its sporting origins and began to be used in a variety of contexts, from business to personal situations. The transition in meaning likely stemmed from the concept of demonstrating control, authority, or foresight in a given situation.

Example Sentence

"In our team meetings, it's usually the project manager who calls the shots, deciding the priorities and delegating tasks."

The idiom "call the shots" underscores the notion of authority and decision-making. It serves as a metaphor for taking charge, demonstrating leadership, or exerting influence. Whether in a corporate boardroom, on a film set, or within a family dynamic, the ability to "call the shots" often implies a level of respect, responsibility, and trust that has been granted to or earned by an individual.

Play by Ear

The idiom "play by ear" has two primary meanings. The first refers to the ability to play a piece of music by just listening to it, without the need for written music. The second, more general meaning, is to handle a situation without a definite plan, improvising as one goes along.

Origin

1. Musical Origins: The idiom has direct ties to musicians, particularly those who can listen to a piece of music and then reproduce it on their instrument without referencing sheet music. This skill, while innate for some, can also be cultivated over time. Such musicians are said to "play by ear."

2. Contrast to Formal Learning: Playing by ear stands in contrast to the more formalized method of learning music through notation. Some musicians, especially those in oral traditions or those who engage in genres that value improvisation, often develop a keen ability to play by ear.

3. Extension to General Use: The idiom's meaning broadened beyond the realm of music to describe any situation where someone might proceed without a set plan or without standard preparation, choosing instead to rely on intuition, experience, or improvisation.

Example Sentence

"Since we don't have a set itinerary for our trip, we'll just play it by ear and decide what to do each day."

The phrase "play by ear" encapsulates the idea of flexibility and adaptability. It speaks to the ability to navigate unfamiliar or changing situations with confidence and skill, even in the absence of clear instructions or a predefined path. Whether in the realm of music or in daily life, to "play by ear" is to embrace the unknown and to trust in one's abilities to adapt and respond effectively.

Level Playing Field

Meaning

The idiom "level playing field" refers to a situation where all participants have an equal chance of succeeding, usually because no external advantages or disadvantages are given to any party. It emphasizes fairness and equality of opportunity, ensuring that no individual or group has an unfair edge over others.

Origin

1. Sports Origins: The concept derives from sports, particularly those played on fields like football, soccer, or rugby. For these games, it's critical for the field to be level, ensuring that neither side has a terrain-based advantage or disadvantage. A field tilted in one direction would inherently benefit one team over the other.

2. Extension into Broader Contexts: As sports often serve as metaphors for life and business, the idea of a "level playing field" was adopted into broader contexts. It became synonymous with fairness in competition, whether in business, politics, or other areas.

3. Modern Connotations: With discussions on social equality, economic disparities, and access to opportunities becoming more prominent, the term is frequently used to describe situations where systemic biases might give certain groups advantages over others. Ensuring a "level playing field" in such contexts means removing these biases to provide equal opportunities for all.

Example Sentence

"To ensure that all students have an equal chance at success, the school district is working to create a level playing field by providing resources and support to underfunded schools."

The phrase "level playing field" embodies the values of fairness and equality. It stands as a reminder that true competition and achievement arise not from artificial advantages but from genuine skill, effort, and merit. In a broader societal context, advocating for a "level playing field" pushes for the dismantling of systemic barriers and the championing of equal opportunities for all, irrespective of their backgrounds or circumstances.

Have Skin in the Game

The idiom "have skin in the game" refers to having a personal investment or stake in a particular venture, project, or endeavor. This personal investment can be in the form of money, time, effort, or reputation. The implication is that when someone has "skin in the game," they are more committed, engaged, and likely to be concerned about the outcome because they stand to gain or lose based on its success or failure.

Origin

1. Gambling Associations: One theory suggests the phrase has its roots in gambling, where players bet actual money – their "skin" – on the outcome of a game. If they don't place a bet, they have no personal stake in the game's outcome.

2. Business and Investing: The term gained broader usage in the world of business and investing. Investors or business owners who put their own money into a venture can be said to have "skin in the game" because they stand to personally benefit or suffer from the business's success or failure.

3. Popularized by Nassim Nicholas Taleb: The Lebanese-American scholar and statistician Nassim Nicholas Taleb further popularized the term in his writings, emphasizing the importance of decision-makers bearing the risks of their decisions, ensuring alignment between risk and reward.

Example Sentence

"When the CEO invested a significant portion of his personal savings into the new company initiative, employees recognized that he truly had skin in the game and was committed to its success."

The phrase "have skin in the game" underscores the importance of personal commitment and the alignment of incentives. It suggests that those who stand to gain or lose from the outcome of a situation are more likely to be genuinely committed to its success. In both business and broader life situations, having "skin in the game" acts as a motivator, encouraging individuals to act with greater responsibility, diligence, and integrity.

All Fair in Love and War

Meaning

The idiom "all's fair in love and war" suggests that in certain situations, people are allowed or even expected to behave in ways that would normally be considered unacceptable. Specifically, in the realms of love and conflict, the usual rules of conduct may not apply, and behavior that's otherwise seen as unfair becomes justifiable.

Origin

1. Literary Roots: The first known use of this phrase in English is by poet John Lyly in his work "Euphues: The Anatomy of Wit" published in 1578: "The rules of fair play do not apply in love and war." The phrase became more popular and recognizable in its current form, "all's fair in love and war," as it was used in literature and discourse throughout the subsequent centuries.

2. Context of Love and War: Both love and war are domains where emotions run high and stakes are significant. In matters of the heart, people might engage in elaborate gestures, games of jealousy, or other tactics to win over their desired partner. Similarly, in war, the objective of winning sometimes overshadows the usual ethical considerations.

3. Philosophical Discussions: The phrase has spurred philosophical debates over time, with some arguing that ethics shouldn't be suspended in any situation, while others believe that there are circumstances where the ends justify the means.

Example Sentence

"He knew he was being sneaky by sending anonymous gifts to win her affection, but as they say, all's fair in love and war."

The idiom "all's fair in love and war" encapsulates the idea that intense situations, whether they're matters of the heart or conflicts on the battlefield, may call for unconventional or even drastic measures. However, the phrase is often used with a hint of irony, recognizing that while such actions might be understandable given the circumstances, they aren't necessarily endorsed or seen as entirely above board. It's a reminder of the lengths people might go to when they're deeply passionate or desperate about a cause or a person.

Throw a Curveball

The idiom "throw a curveball" refers to introducing an unexpected challenge, problem, or deviation from what is standard or expected. It's used when someone or something changes in a way that is unexpected, often creating a challenge or requiring a change in plans.

Origin

1. Baseball Origins: The phrase has its roots in the sport of baseball. A curveball is a type of pitch thrown with a specific grip and wrist movement that causes the ball to have a curved trajectory. Batters often find it challenging to hit because of its unexpected and deceptive movement, making it deviate from the straight path they might be expecting.

2. Metaphorical Extension: Over time, this baseball term began to be used metaphorically in everyday language. Just as a batter can be caught off guard by a curveball, so too can people in real life be surprised or challenged by unexpected events or situations.

3. Popularity in Culture: The universality of baseball, especially in the United States, and the relatable nature of the unexpected challenges in life, made the phrase popular and easily understood in various contexts.

Example Sentence

"I had everything planned for the outdoor event, but the sudden rainstorm threw a curveball, and we had to adjust quickly."

The idiom "throw a curveball" captures the unpredictable nature of life and how, even with the best-laid plans, there can always be unforeseen challenges or changes. It serves as a reminder to always be adaptable and prepared for the unexpected. In a broader sense, the phrase speaks to the human experience of dealing with sudden obstacles, emphasizing resilience and the need to be nimble in response to changing circumstances. Whether in personal life, professional settings, or broader societal contexts, "throw a curveball" is a testament to the ever-changing nature of reality and our need to navigate it skillfully.

Buzzer Beater

The term "buzzer beater" refers to a shot in basketball that is taken just before the game or quarter buzzer sounds and counts if it goes into the basket. It's a moment of high drama, as the outcome of the game can hinge on that last-second shot. In a broader sense, the term is used outside of sports to describe any action or event that occurs at the last possible moment.

Origin

1. Basketball Roots: Originating from basketball, the term describes one of the most exciting moments in the sport. As the clock ticks down, players often rush to take a shot before time runs out. If the shot is successful and made before the buzzer sounds, it's a "buzzer beater."

2. Symbol of Drama and Timeliness: The thrill and tension associated with such a crucial moment in the game made the term memorable. As a result, it became synonymous with last-minute actions or decisions in various contexts, not just basketball.

3. Adoption in Popular Culture: Its dramatic nature made "buzzer beater" a popular term even outside of sports, capturing the essence of last-second victories or decisions in movies, TV shows, and other forms of media.

Example Sentence

"I thought I was going to miss the deadline, but I managed a buzzer beater and submitted the report just in time."

The idiom "buzzer beater" encapsulates the tension and thrill of last-minute actions, whether in sports or everyday life. It speaks to the human capacity for pulling through under pressure, often in situations where every second counts. The term also underscores the importance of timeliness and the satisfaction derived from achieving something right at the wire. Whether facing deadlines, making important decisions, or simply trying to win a game, the concept of the "buzzer beater" serves as a metaphorical representation of dramatic, last-second success.

Play Second Fiddle

To "play second fiddle" means to take on a subordinate role or be regarded as less important than someone else. It implies being in a supporting or secondary position rather than being the main focus or leader in a particular situation.

Origin

1. Musical Origins: The idiom has its roots in the world of music, specifically in orchestras. In a typical orchestra, the first violinist or "first fiddle" plays the lead role, often getting the most significant or prominent parts of a composition. The "second fiddle," while still crucial, plays a more supportive or accompanying role.

2. Hierarchy of Roles: In many orchestras, the first violinist is considered the leader, or concertmaster, having achieved that position through a combination of skill, experience, and sometimes through competitions. They often get solos and are more prominently featured. The second violinists, though talented and vital for the orchestra's overall sound, do not get as much individual attention.

3. Broadening of the Term: Over time, the term moved beyond the realm of music to describe any situation where one person or entity is overshadowed by or subservient to another.

Example Sentence

"Although she was talented, she always felt like she played second fiddle to her older sister."

The idiom "play second fiddle" delves into the human experience of comparison, hierarchy, and the desire for recognition. It underscores the dynamics present not just in musical ensembles, but in families, workplaces, and various social settings. Everyone, at some point in their lives, has felt like they've played second fiddle, whether it's to a sibling, a coworker, or even to societal expectations. The phrase serves as a poignant reminder of the importance of recognizing and valuing everyone's contributions, irrespective of their position or rank.

Change the Game

The idiom "change the game" refers to doing something that alters the usual methods or rules, often in a significant and innovative manner. It signifies introducing new strategies, ideas, or products that completely redefine the standards or expectations in a particular field or situation.

Origin

1. Sports Origins: The phrase is believed to have originated from the world of sports, where a particular play, strategy, or player can literally change the outcome of a game. An innovative tactic or an unexpected play can alter the dynamics of a competition.

2. Innovation and Business: As the term evolved, it began to be used in business and technology sectors. Here, it is often used to describe a product, service, or idea that disrupts the status quo, reshaping an industry or market.

3. Cultural Significance: Beyond its literal origins, the phrase encapsulates the idea of revolutionizing a system or process. This idea has been embraced culturally to highlight groundbreaking changes or to challenge traditional ways of thinking.

Example Sentence

"When smartphones were first introduced, they completely changed the game for the mobile industry."

The idiom "change the game" is a testament to the power of innovation and adaptability. In an ever-evolving world, the phrase serves as a reminder of the significance of continuous improvement and the potential for groundbreaking ideas to redefine the known landscape. Whether in the context of business, technology, culture, or personal endeavors, "change the game" underscores the importance of staying ahead of the curve and embracing change.

In the Home Stretch

Meaning

The idiom "in the home stretch" refers to being in the final phase or nearing the end of a task, project, competition, or journey. When someone says they are "in the home stretch," it implies that most of the work or distance has been covered, and only a small portion remains to be completed or traversed.

Origin

1. Horse Racing Origins: The phrase has its roots in horse racing. In a race, the "home stretch" is the final straight section of the track leading to the finish line. It's the last and often the most crucial part of the race where the outcome is determined.

2. Visual Imagery: The vivid imagery of a racer giving their all in this last section, with the end in sight, became a popular metaphor for anyone nearing the completion of a task or endeavor.

3. Broadened Use: Over time, the term has been adopted outside of racing to refer to the concluding stages of various events or tasks, emphasizing the anticipation and culmination of efforts.

Example Sentence

"We've been working on this project for months, and now that we're in the home stretch, everyone is excited to see the final results."

The idiom "in the home stretch" evokes a sense of anticipation, culmination, and sometimes relief. It resonates with the shared human experience of seeing the fruits of one's labor after prolonged effort. In both personal and professional contexts, the phrase serves as a reminder of the persistence and resilience required to navigate challenges and approach the finish line, whatever that may represent in one's journey. Whether tackling a long-term project, facing a challenge, or embarking on a personal endeavor, "in the home stretch" speaks to the universal thrill of nearing a much-anticipated conclusion.

Drop the Ball

Meaning

The idiom "drop the ball" means to make a mistake, especially by failing to take action or to handle a responsibility correctly. When someone is accused of "dropping the ball," it implies negligence, oversight, or a lapse in judgment or responsibility on their part.

Origin

1. Sports Reference: The phrase is believed to have originated from sports, particularly American football, where dropping the ball can disrupt a play and result in missed opportunities or even turnovers to the opposing team. Such an error in the game can have significant consequences for the team's performance.

2. Visual Imagery: The act of physically dropping a ball can be seen as a sudden, unanticipated error. This visual representation of a mishap translates well into describing mistakes in various contexts, from professional to personal.

3. Broadened Use: Over the years, this sports-derived phrase began to be applied more broadly to any situation where an individual failed to meet expectations, neglected a duty, or made an error in judgment.

Example Sentence

"She was supposed to send the report by noon, but she dropped the ball and forgot, causing a delay in the meeting."

The idiom "drop the ball" underscores the importance of responsibility and vigilance. In many scenarios, tasks or duties are like metaphorical balls being juggled, and a single oversight can have cascading consequences. This phrase serves as a reminder of the accountability one holds in various roles, from professional responsibilities to personal commitments. Whether it's managing multiple tasks at work, upholding promises in relationships, or maintaining commitments, "drop the ball" underscores the need for attention to detail and reliability in various spheres of life.

210

Cover Your Bases

The idiom "cover your bases" means to ensure that all possible actions or contingencies are taken care of, to be fully prepared for any potential scenarios, or to take precautions against every potential challenge or difficulty.

Origin

1. Baseball Influence: The phrase is commonly believed to have originated from baseball. In baseball, defensive players aim to "cover" or guard each base to prevent the opposing team's players from safely reaching them. When all bases are covered, it minimizes the chances of the other team scoring.

2. Military Strategy: Another interpretation links the idiom to military strategy, where it's crucial to protect or "cover" all bases or strongholds to prevent enemy infiltration or attacks.

3. General Adaptation: Over time, this sports and potentially military term was adapted to general use, symbolizing the importance of preparedness in various contexts.

Example Sentence

"Before launching the marketing campaign, we need to cover our bases and ensure we've considered all feedback and potential market reactions."

The idiom "cover your bases" embodies the essence of thorough preparation and anticipation. Whether in a game, business endeavor, or personal project, the idea is to minimize vulnerabilities and maximize the chances of success. It's a reminder that foresight, comprehensive planning, and attention to potential pitfalls can be invaluable assets. When one seeks to "cover their bases," they're embodying a proactive approach, ensuring they're ready for whatever challenges or opportunities arise, thus enhancing the potential for success and minimizing unexpected negative outcomes.

The Gloves Are Off

The idiom "the gloves are off" suggests that someone is ready to engage in an open confrontation, dispute, or fight without holding back. It implies that the niceties or restraints once in place are now abandoned, and the parties involved are prepared to handle the situation aggressively or without decorum.

Origin

1. Boxing Origins: The phrase has roots in the sport of boxing. In traditional boxing, gloves are worn to provide some protection to the fighters. When a boxer removes their gloves, it symbolizes a more brutal or bare-knuckle form of fighting, where the hits can be more damaging, and there's a greater risk of injury.

2. Symbolism of Protection: The act of wearing gloves in many contexts—be it boxing, manual labor, or handling delicate items—often signifies protection, either to the wearer or to the object being handled. Removing gloves can symbolize the removal of that protection, leading to a more direct or unmediated interaction.

3. Shift to Broader Usage: Over time, the phrase was adopted into general colloquial speech and began to be used in contexts outside of physical combat. It evolved to describe any situation where individuals or groups were no longer playing nice or adhering to the usual rules or courtesies, whether in politics, business negotiations, or personal disputes.

Example Sentence

"When negotiations broke down between the two companies, it was clear that the gloves were off, and both sides began launching public criticisms against each other."

"The gloves are off" captures the essence of a shift from courteous, rule-bound interactions to direct, unfiltered confrontations. It speaks to those moments in human dynamics when decorum is set aside, and parties are ready to defend their positions fiercely. Whether in a boardroom or on a personal front, the idiom marks the transition from a measured approach to a no-holds-barred attitude.

Mythical Creatures and Folklore

Chase a Unicorn

Meaning

The idiom "chase a unicorn" refers to the act of pursuing an idea or goal that is fanciful, unrealistic, or unattainable. Just as unicorns are mythical creatures and elusive in nature, chasing after one metaphorically suggests going after something that is likely out of reach or doesn't exist in the first place.

Origin

1. Mythological Context: Unicorns are legendary creatures that have been a part of folklore and mythology for centuries. They are often depicted as horse-like animals with a single spiral horn projecting from their forehead. Despite being fictional, they have often been the subject of hunts and quests in myths and legends.

2. Renaissance and Middle Ages: During these periods, unicorns were believed to be real and were symbols of purity and grace. Their horns, sometimes referred to as alicorns, were believed to have magical properties, including the ability to neutralize poisons. This led to a high demand for "unicorn horns," which were often just narwhal tusks sold at high prices. The hunt for these horns can be seen as a literal chase for unicorns.

3. Modern Usage: In contemporary times, especially in the business and tech world, a "unicorn" is also a term used to describe a start-up company valued at over $1 billion. The term indicates rarity, as such startups are as uncommon as the mythical creature. This modern use further solidifies the idiom's association with rarity and the pursuit of the exceptional.

Example Sentence

"While innovation is essential, it's important for the team not to chase unicorns and instead focus on achievable, realistic goals."

The idiom "chase a unicorn" encapsulates the human tendency to sometimes get lost in the allure of the unattainable or the exceptional. It's a cautionary phrase, reminding individuals that while ambition and dreams are crucial, it's equally vital to remain grounded and pragmatic. Pursuits based on illusions or misconceptions can lead to wasted efforts and disappointments. Thus, while it's noble to aim high, "chasing a unicorn" warns of the pitfalls of losing oneself in unrealistic or unattainable fantasies.

215

Dragon's Breath

The idiom "dragon's breath" typically refers to a person's extremely bad breath, comparable to the fiery, foul breath of a mythical dragon. Additionally, it can also be used metaphorically to describe anything extremely hot or intense.

Origin

1. Mythological Context: Dragons are legendary creatures that appear in the folklore of many cultures around the world. They are often depicted as large, serpent-like creatures that breathe fire. In many tales, dragons are fearsome beasts, and their fiery breath is one of their most dangerous weapons.

2. Literary Depictions: In literature, dragons and their fiery breath have been used to represent numerous challenges that heroes must overcome. The idea of a dragon's breath being powerful and overwhelming has made it a staple in many stories and legends.

3. Comparison to Foul Breath: The association between foul breath and a dragon's powerful, noxious exhalation is a hyperbolic comparison. By likening someone's bad breath to that of a dragon, the idiom emphasizes the intensity and unpleasantness of the odor.

4. Culinary Context: Separately, "Dragon's Breath" is also the name given to a dessert made of cereal puffs infused with liquid nitrogen. When consumed, it produces a smoke-like vapor from the eater's nose and mouth, mimicking a dragon exhaling smoke.

Example Sentence

"After he woke up in the morning, his dragon's breath was so strong that it could have woken the entire house."

The idiom "dragon's breath" taps into the long-standing human fascination with mythical creatures and the attributes ascribed to them. By equating foul breath to the fiery exhalation of a dragon, the phrase not only emphasizes the potency of the odor but also adds a touch of humor to an otherwise embarrassing situation. In broader uses, "dragon's breath" can effectively convey the idea of something being intensely strong, hot, or overwhelming, echoing the formidable nature of the legendary beast.

Herculean Task

The idiom "Herculean task" refers to a task or challenge that is extremely difficult and requires great strength, effort, or resources to complete. It suggests an endeavor that is daunting, perhaps seemingly impossible, but is undertaken with determination.

Origin

1. Greek Mythology: The term "Herculean" is derived from Hercules (or Heracles, as he is known in Greek mythology), who was a legendary hero celebrated for his incredible strength and for the twelve labors he was commanded to perform as penance for a crime. These labors included slaying the Nemean lion, capturing the Golden Hind, and cleaning the Augean stables in a single day.

2. Symbolism of the Labors: Each of Hercules' twelve labors was considered impossible for any mortal. Yet, with wit, strength, and persistence, Hercules accomplished each one. His feats became synonymous with overcoming insurmountable odds.

3. Transition to Modern Language: As tales of Hercules' deeds spread, his name became emblematic of immense strength and determination. The term "Herculean" was eventually adopted into the English language to describe anything that required extraordinary effort or strength.

Example Sentence

"Organizing the international conference, with thousands of participants from all over the world, was a Herculean task, but the team managed it brilliantly."

The idiom "Herculean task" serves as both a recognition of the difficulty of a particular challenge and a nod to the potential of human determination and ingenuity. While a Herculean task may seem overwhelming at first, invoking the name of Hercules also carries with it the inspiration that, with enough effort and persistence, even the most challenging obstacles can be overcome. The phrase is a testament to the enduring power of mythology and its ability to provide frameworks for understanding and describing the human experience.

Achilles' Heel

The idiom "Achilles' heel" refers to a person's weakness or vulnerability, despite overall strength. This weakness can lead to downfall or failure. It points out that even the strongest or most invincible person or entity has some vulnerability.

Origin

1. Greek Mythology: This phrase has its roots in the story of Achilles, a hero in Greek mythology. As a baby, Achilles was dipped into the River Styx by his mother, Thetis, to make him invulnerable. The water would grant invincibility to any part of the body it touched. However, she held him by his heel, so that part did not touch the water and remained vulnerable. Years later, during the Trojan War, Achilles was fatally wounded in the heel by an arrow shot by Paris, leading to his death.

2. Symbolism of the Story: The tale of Achilles underscores the idea that everyone has some weakness, no matter how invincible they might appear on the surface. The concept of an invulnerable hero with a single weak point is a powerful narrative tool and a commentary on the human condition.

3. Transition to Modern Language: The term "Achilles' heel" was eventually adopted into the English language as a metaphor for a vulnerability or weak spot, drawing directly from the mythological story of Achilles.

Example Sentence

"Despite being the top-selling product in the company's lineup, its poor battery life was its Achilles' heel, leading to many customer complaints."

The idiom "Achilles' heel" underscores the idea that everyone and everything has a vulnerability. It reminds us that no matter how strong, talented, or skilled someone might be, there's often a hidden weak point. Recognizing our own "Achilles' heel" can be a path to personal growth, while identifying it in others or in systems can be a strategic advantage. The phrase emphasizes the importance of understanding not just strengths, but also weaknesses, and it's a vivid example of how ancient myths can provide language for modern concepts.

Witching Hour

The term "witching hour" traditionally refers to a specific time at night, usually around midnight, when supernatural events, such as the appearance of ghosts, witches, or other paranormal entities, are believed to be at their peak. In more modern usage, especially in the context of parenting, it can also refer to a period in the late afternoon or early evening when babies and young children become fussy or have difficulty sleeping.

Origin

1. Medieval Beliefs: During the medieval times in Europe, it was widely believed that the powers of evil were stronger at certain times. Midnight, being the transition between days, was seen as a particularly potent time for dark magic and supernatural occurrences.

2. Witchcraft: Witches were believed to hold their meetings, known as "sabbats", during the witching hour. The late hour was ideal for such secret gatherings, as most townspeople would be asleep, allowing witches to carry out their activities undisturbed.

3. Cultural Evolution: As supernatural beliefs became part of folklore and popular stories, the idea of the witching hour became more ingrained in the cultural consciousness. Over time, the term began to be used in literature, film, and other media to denote a time of heightened supernatural activity.

4. Modern Parenting Context: More recently, the term has been co-opted by parents and caregivers to describe the fussy period many infants and toddlers go through during the late afternoon or early evening, often characterized by persistent crying or discomfort.

Example Sentence

"In the old haunted mansion, strange noises and apparitions were most frequently reported during the witching hour."

The concept of the "witching hour" touches on humanity's longstanding fascination with the supernatural and the unseen. It embodies the mysteries of the night and the primal fears associated with the unknown. Whether referencing ancient beliefs in witchcraft or the modern challenges of parenting, the phrase evokes a sense of unease and heightened awareness, a time when the ordinary rules might not apply and when one should be on guard for the unexpected.

Unicorn Syndrome

Meaning

The term "unicorn syndrome" isn't a widely recognized idiom in the same traditional sense as many others. However, in contemporary contexts, particularly in the business world and the dating realm, a "unicorn" often refers to something or someone that is highly desirable but difficult to find or obtain. The "unicorn syndrome" typically refers to the belief or delusion that such a rare and perfect entity exists, and the ensuing pursuit of this often unrealistic ideal. In business, it can refer to a start-up company valued at over one billion dollars.

Origin

1. Mythical Creature: The unicorn is a legendary creature that has been described since antiquity as a beast with a single large, spiraled horn projecting from its forehead. Over centuries, it has come to symbolize purity, beauty, and rarity.

2. Modern Tech Industry: In the technology startup world, venture capitalist Aileen Lee coined the term "unicorn" in 2013 to describe start-ups valued at $1 billion or more, emphasizing their rarity.

3. Dating and Relationships: In polyamorous communities, a "unicorn" refers to a bisexual person (usually a woman) who is willing to join an existing couple. Their rarity gives rise to the term. In a broader context, it can also refer to the ideal partner that someone might be searching for, even though such a perfect person doesn't exist.

4. Pursuit of Perfection: The "syndrome" aspect of the phrase captures the obsessive quest for something rare and perfect – whether it's the perfect partner, the ideal employee, or another form of idealized pursuit.

Example Sentence

"After interviewing dozens of candidates and rejecting them for minor reasons, the HR manager realized she might be suffering from unicorn syndrome, expecting to find a candidate that simply didn't exist."

The "unicorn syndrome" reflects modern society's aspirations for perfection and the best of the best, whether in personal relationships, professional pursuits, or other areas of life. It highlights the challenges and pitfalls of chasing after an often unattainable or nonexistent ideal. The term serves as a reminder that while striving for the best is commendable, it's also essential to manage expectations and be realistic about what's attainable.

Siren's Song

Meaning

The idiom "siren's song" refers to an alluring or tempting appeal, often leading to a dangerous or detrimental situation. It describes something that seems very appealing but might lead to negative consequences if pursued.

Origin

1. Greek Mythology: The concept of the siren's song originates from ancient Greek mythology. Sirens were mythical creatures, often depicted as women with bird-like features, who lived on islands and sang enchanting songs. Their mesmerizing melodies lured sailors towards them, causing the sailors' ships to crash on the rocks surrounding the sirens' islands.

2. Homer's Odyssey: One of the most famous references to sirens can be found in Homer's "Odyssey". In this epic, the hero Odysseus and his crew encounter the sirens during their journey home. Forewarned by the sorceress Circe about the deadly allure of the sirens' song, Odysseus orders his men to plug their ears with beeswax. Curious to hear the song himself without succumbing to its allure, Odysseus has himself tied to the ship's mast. As they pass the sirens, Odysseus is enchanted by their song and demands to be released, but his crew, unable to hear the song, continue sailing past, saving themselves from destruction.

3. Metaphoric Evolution: Over time, the term "siren's song" began to be used metaphorically. It came to represent any alluring temptation that might lead one into harm or trouble.

Example Sentence

"Many investors were drawn to the siren's song of quick profits in the stock market, only to suffer significant losses when the bubble burst."

The idiom "siren's song" captures the tension between attraction and danger. It underscores the human vulnerability to temptation, especially when faced with something seemingly irresistible. The phrase serves as a cautionary note, reminding individuals to be wary of things that seem too good to be true and to consider potential consequences before being lured into potentially perilous situations. Whether in matters of the heart, finance, or personal decisions, the siren's song warns of the risks that come with succumbing to seductive but hazardous temptations.

Phoenix Rising

Meaning

The idiom "phoenix rising" or "rise like a phoenix" refers to being reborn, rejuvenated, or renewed after experiencing destruction, defeat, or failure. It is used to describe something or someone that emerges stronger, better, or more powerful after experiencing adversity or near-obliteration.

Origin

1. Ancient Mythology: The concept of the phoenix originates from ancient Greek and Egyptian mythology. The phoenix is a legendary bird that, upon dying or being consumed by flames, is reborn from its ashes. Its life cycle involves death and rebirth, making it a symbol of renewal, resurrection, and eternal life.

2. Symbolic Representation: Throughout history, the phoenix has been a symbol of regeneration, resilience, and the cyclical nature of life. Many cultures, from the Greeks and Romans to the Chinese and Japanese, have stories or legends about birds resembling the phoenix and its regenerative qualities.

3. Literary References: The phoenix has been referenced in various literary works over centuries, from classical texts to modern literature. For example, in William Shakespeare's play "Henry VIII", the phoenix's rebirth from its ashes is used as a metaphor for Anne Boleyn's rise after Catherine of Aragon's fall.

Example Sentence

"After the company went bankrupt due to mismanagement, it made a dramatic comeback under new leadership, truly like a phoenix rising from the ashes."

The idiom "phoenix rising" encapsulates the idea of transformation, resilience, and the ability to bounce back from setbacks. It serves as a powerful reminder that, even in the face of overwhelming challenges, individuals or entities can undergo rebirth and experience new beginnings. The imagery of the phoenix, with its fiery end and subsequent rebirth, resonates with the human spirit's ability to overcome adversity and reminds us of the potential for renewal even after the darkest times.

Beware of Greeks Bearing Gifts

Meaning

The idiom "Beware of Greeks bearing gifts" is a cautionary statement, advising against trusting enemies or those who appear to be offering favors or gifts with ulterior motives. In essence, it suggests skepticism towards seemingly generous actions from potentially dubious sources.

Origin

1. Ancient Trojan War: The phrase originates from the ancient Greek and Roman legends about the Trojan War. According to the legend, after a decade-long siege of Troy by the Greeks, the Greeks devised a plan to infiltrate the city by constructing a massive wooden horse, known as the Trojan Horse. They left the horse at the gates of Troy as a supposed peace offering or gift, and then pretended to sail away.

2. The Trojan Horse: The Trojans, believing they had won the war and that the horse was a gift to the gods, brought the wooden horse into their fortified city. Unbeknownst to them, Greek soldiers were hidden inside the horse. At night, the Greek soldiers emerged, opened the gates for the Greek army (which had returned under the cover of darkness), leading to the fall of Troy.

3. Literary Record: The Latin version of the caution, "Timeo Danaos et dona ferentes," is found in Virgil's "Aeneid." It translates to "I fear the Greeks, even those bearing gifts." The phrase is spoken by Laocoön, a priest who tried to warn the Trojans against bringing the wooden horse into their city.

Example Sentence

"When the rival company offered to help us out during our financial crisis, my first thought was, 'Beware of Greeks bearing gifts.'"

The idiom "Beware of Greeks bearing gifts" serves as a warning against naivety and the dangers of accepting seemingly benevolent gestures without questioning the true intentions behind them. It underscores the age-old understanding that things that seem too good to be true often are and that caution is necessary when dealing with situations that appear unexpectedly favorable.

Midas Touch

The idiom "Midas touch" refers to the ability to turn any venture into a success or to make money easily; it's often used to describe someone who seems to succeed in every project they undertake or has a knack for making profitable decisions. The term is generally used in a positive sense, though it can occasionally carry the implication of greed or the consequences of unchecked ambition.

Origin

1. Greek Mythology: The origin of this phrase can be traced back to the tale of King Midas of Phrygia. According to Greek mythology, Midas was granted a wish by the god Dionysus, and he wished that everything he touched would turn to gold. At first, this gift seemed to be a blessing as objects, fruits, and other items turned to gold upon his touch, making him immensely wealthy.

2. The Curse: However, the blessing soon turned into a curse when Midas realized that he couldn't touch his daughter or even food and water without them turning to gold. This story ends in tragedy, with Midas recognizing the consequences of his unchecked greed and wishing to reverse his golden touch. Dionysus grants this request, and Midas learns a valuable lesson about the true value of life versus material wealth.

3. Evolution of the Phrase: Over time, the term "Midas touch" made its way into English vernacular, symbolizing the ability to effortlessly turn any venture into a success, especially in financial terms. However, while the modern idiom often lacks the cautionary undertones of the original tale, its roots in the story of King Midas serve as a reminder of the potential pitfalls of unchecked ambition and greed.

Example Sentence

"Everything she invests in seems to prosper; she truly has the Midas touch."

The idiom "Midas touch" encapsulates the notion of success, especially in financial undertakings. While it celebrates prosperity and the seemingly magical ability to generate wealth, its mythological origins also hint at the potential dangers of valuing gold over genuine human connections. As with many idioms rooted in ancient tales, "Midas touch" not only provides a shorthand for success but also offers a deeper reflection on the values and priorities that drive our decisions.

Banshee Wail

Meaning

The idiom "Banshee wail" or "wail like a banshee" is used to describe a loud, piercing scream or cry, often filled with distress, anguish, or pain. The term can be used to describe both literal screams and metaphorically to depict strong emotions or reactions.

Origin

1. Irish Folklore: The phrase originates from Irish and Scottish mythology. A banshee (from the Irish "bean sídhe" meaning "woman of the fairy mounds" or simply "fairy woman") is a supernatural being, often depicted as a female spirit or fairy. She is believed to appear and wail, shriek, or keen before someone dies as an omen or warning of their impending death.

2. Characteristics of the Banshee: Banshees are typically described as wearing red or green, with long, disheveled hair. They might appear as a young beautiful woman, a stately matron, or a raddled old hag. The common thread among the various depictions is the mournful, haunting cry they emit, signaling a death in the family of those who hear it.

3. Cultural Spread: The legends of banshees are deeply rooted in Celtic folklore, but with the migration of the Irish and Scots to other parts of the world, especially the United States, the tales of the banshee and her eerie wail became more widely recognized and entered into the broader English lexicon.

Example Sentence

"After dropping the plate, Jenny let out a banshee wail, alerting everyone in the house to the accident."

The idiom "Banshee wail" taps into the chilling and haunting aspects of folklore, underscoring intense emotional outbursts or reactions. The banshee, with her foreboding lament, serves as a cultural symbol for strong emotional expression, especially sorrow or fear. When someone is described as wailing like a banshee, it invokes images of not just the volume but also the profound emotion behind the sound.

Open Pandora's Box

To "open Pandora's box" means to take an action that seems small or innocent, but that turns out to have severely detrimental and far-reaching consequences. It is used to suggest that one small act or decision can lead to a cascade of events or problems that were previously unknown or kept in check.

Origin

1. Greek Mythology: The phrase originates from ancient Greek mythology. According to the myth, Pandora was the first human woman created by the gods. She was given a box (or in some versions, a jar) as a gift from Zeus, the king of the gods, with strict instructions never to open it.

2. Zeus's Revenge: The box was Zeus's revenge on humanity after Prometheus stole fire from the gods and gave it to humans. Curiosity overcame Pandora and she eventually opened the box, releasing all the evils of the world, such as disease, sorrow, and despair. Only one thing remained inside once she hurriedly closed it again: hope.

3. Symbolism: Over time, the tale has been used to illustrate the unforeseen consequences of one's actions and the inherent dangers of unchecked curiosity. The act of opening the box is symbolic of initiating a chain reaction of unintended troubles.

4. Modern Interpretation: In contemporary discussions, the phrase can also be used to refer to uncovering something complex or getting to the root of a problem, often with the implication that doing so might be a double-edged sword.

Example Sentence

"By digging into the company's financial records, the auditor opened Pandora's box, revealing years of fraud and embezzlement."

The idiom "Open Pandora's Box" serves as a cautionary expression, warning individuals of the unintended and often overwhelming consequences that might arise from a seemingly simple or innocent act. The legend of Pandora reminds us of the human traits of curiosity and the unforeseen repercussions it can usher in, while also offering a glimmer of hope even in the face of adversity.

Pegasus in Flight

While not a standard idiom, the imagery of "Pegasus in Flight" could symbolize inspiration, freedom, transcendence, or elevation above earthly concerns. Pegasus is often associated with poetry and the arts, and its flight might represent the soaring of creativity or imagination.

Origin

1. Greek Mythology: Pegasus is a winged divine horse usually depicted as pure white in color. He was born from the blood of Medusa when she was beheaded by the hero Perseus. Pegasus is best known for his association with the Muses and Mount Helicon, where he struck the ground with his hoof, causing the Hippocrene spring, sacred to the Muses, to emerge.

2. Symbol of Inspiration: In mythology, Pegasus was caught by the Greek hero Bellerophon, with the assistance of Athena and Poseidon. Pegasus allowed Bellerophon to ride him in order to defeat the monstrous Chimera. However, when Bellerophon tried to fly to Mount Olympus, he was thrown off by Pegasus and fell to his death. The act of Pegasus flying solo to Olympus signifies rising above human limitations or hubris.

3. Modern Interpretation: Over the years, Pegasus has been a symbol of wisdom and fame, especially in poetic inspiration. Its image has been used in emblems, company logos, and literature to symbolize a range of positive attributes like speed, power, and flight.

Example Sentence

"As the musicians played, it felt like a Pegasus in flight, lifting the spirits of everyone in the room, transporting them to another realm."

While "Pegasus in Flight" might not be a conventional idiom, its rich mythological background makes it a potent metaphorical expression. It could represent the pinnacle of achievement, the epitome of inspiration, or the act of breaking through boundaries to reach new heights.

The Trojan Horse

The idiom "The Trojan Horse" refers to any trick or stratagem that causes a target to invite a foe into a securely protected place or to accept something that will later harm or destroy them. In a broader context, it signifies deception or subterfuge that leads one to unwittingly allow an enemy into their midst.

Origin

1. Ancient Greek Epic: The term originates from the ancient Greek story of the wooden horse that was used by the Greeks to enter the city of Troy and win the Trojan War. The Trojan Horse is a tale from the Trojan War, as told in Virgil's Latin epic poem "The Aeneid" and also mentioned in the "Odyssey" by Homer.

2. The Deceptive Strategy: According to the story, after a fruitless 10-year siege of Troy, the Greeks constructed a giant wooden horse and hid a select group of soldiers inside. The rest of the Greek army then pretended to sail away. The Trojans, believing the war was over, brought the horse into their city as a victory trophy. At night, the Greek soldiers hidden inside the horse emerged, opened the city gates for the returning Greek army, leading to the fall of Troy.

3. Evolution of the Phrase: Over time, the term "Trojan Horse" has come to mean any trick or deception that leads one to allow a foe into a protected place. It's also used in the realm of computer security to describe a type of malicious software that deceives users into willingly running it, only to deliver, once inside the system, a malicious action.

Example Sentence

"Free software downloads from unverified sources can sometimes act as a Trojan Horse, allowing viruses or malware to infiltrate your computer."

The concept of the "Trojan Horse" is a cautionary tale about the dangers of complacency and the importance of vigilance. It's a reminder that threats aren't always overt; they can be hidden or disguised, waiting for the right moment to strike. In a world where deception can be sophisticated and threats can be veiled, the idiom serves as a reminder of the need for discernment and wisdom in our decisions. Whether in personal relationships, business, or digital security, it's always prudent to be wary of things that seem too good to be true.

Gordian Knot

The idiom "Gordian Knot" refers to an extremely complex or difficult problem. The phrase is often used to describe a situation that is very complicated and challenging to solve. To "cut the Gordian Knot" means to solve a difficult problem in a decisive and direct manner, often using an unconventional method.

Origin

1. Ancient Phrygian Legend: The term derives from a legend associated with the Phrygian city of Gordium. According to tradition, Gordius, a peasant who became king of Phrygia, tied a knot with his wagon to a post in such a complex manner that no one could untie it.

2. Oracle's Prophecy: An oracle foretold that the individual who could undo the knot would become the ruler of all Asia. Many tried and failed to untangle the intricate knot.

3. Alexander the Great's Solution: The most famous account of this legend is associated with Alexander the Great. When he visited the city in 333 BC, he was challenged to untie the knot. Unable to find the end to begin unraveling it, he took out his sword and sliced the knot in half with a single stroke, thus providing a direct solution to an intricate problem. This action is where the term "cutting the Gordian Knot" originates.

Example Sentence

"Faced with prolonged legal complications, the CEO decided to cut the Gordian Knot by proposing an out-of-court settlement."

The metaphor of the "Gordian Knot" embodies the essence of challenges that seem insurmountable but can be overcome with creative or bold thinking. It's a testament to human ingenuity and the idea that there's always a solution, no matter how complex the problem might seem. In contemporary usage, it serves as a reminder that sometimes, thinking outside the box or taking decisive action can lead to breakthroughs where traditional methods might falter. Whether faced with a tangled situation in personal matters, business, or broader societal issues, the idiom encourages a proactive and sometimes unconventional approach to problem-solving.

Faustian Bargain

A "Faustian Bargain" refers to a pact or deal in which someone trades something of supreme moral or spiritual importance, such as personal values or the soul, for some worldly or material benefit, such as knowledge, power, or riches. Essentially, it's a deal with the devil — a decision to achieve something you desire but at a great cost.

Origin

1. Johann Wolfgang von Goethe's "Faust": The term has its origins in the legend of Faust, particularly as retold by the German writer Johann Wolfgang von Goethe in his two-part play, "Faust." In Goethe's narrative, Dr. Faust is a disillusioned scholar who, in his desire for more knowledge and pleasures that life has to offer, makes a pact with the devil, Mephistopheles.

2. The Pact: Faust agrees to sell his soul to the devil in exchange for unlimited knowledge and worldly pleasures. However, as the story unfolds, the repercussions of this bargain become clear, leading to Faust's eventual tragic downfall.

3. Earlier Versions of the Tale: While Goethe's rendition is the most renowned, stories of Faust and his devilish pact can be traced back to German folktales, and several versions have been written over the centuries by different authors.

Example Sentence

"In his desire for political power, he made a Faustian Bargain, compromising his core principles and alienating his longtime allies."

The concept of the "Faustian Bargain" is a powerful commentary on the human condition, touching upon themes of ambition, desire, morality, and the consequences of one's choices. In the modern context, the idiom serves as a cautionary tale, warning of the potential dangers of sacrificing one's moral or ethical beliefs for short-term gains. Whether in the realms of business, politics, or personal relationships, the term "Faustian Bargain" acts as a potent reminder that some trades, no matter how tempting, carry costs that can be too heavy to bear.

Mermaid's Tears

Meaning

The term "Mermaid's Tears" isn't as commonly recognized as an idiom in the same way many other phrases are. However, in contemporary times, "Mermaid's Tears" has come to refer to the small plastic pellets (often spherical) used in the manufacture of plastic products. These pellets can sometimes be found on beaches, having washed up from the sea, and are a form of environmental pollution that is dangerous to marine life.

Origin

1. Literary and Mythical Allusions: Mermaids are legendary sea creatures with the upper body of a female human and the tail of a fish. They appear in the folklore of many cultures and are often associated with both beauty and tragedy. Tears shed by such a mythical creature would presumably hold special significance or power.

2. Environmental Concerns: The comparison of these plastic pellets to "mermaid's tears" is symbolic. Just as a mermaid's tear would symbolize the sorrow or pain of the sea, these small bits of plastic pollution represent the harm humans are inflicting on marine environments.

Example Sentence

"While walking along the shoreline, Lily found Mermaid's Tears scattered on the sand, a sad reminder of the impact of plastic pollution on our oceans."

The term "Mermaid's Tears" serves as a poignant metaphor, transforming an everyday industrial material into a symbol of environmental sadness and the ocean's plight. It draws upon myth and legend to create a visceral reaction to an environmental issue, encouraging people to consider the consequences of their actions and the broader impact on the world around them.

Minotaur's Maze

The idiom "Minotaur's Maze" is not a common or standard expression in the English language. However, when used, it could refer to a situation, problem, or place that is extremely complex, confusing, or difficult to navigate, much like the mythical labyrinth that housed the Minotaur in Greek mythology.

Origin

1. Greek Mythology: The Minotaur was a mythical creature with the body of a man and the head of a bull. It was the offspring of Pasiphae and a bull, born as a result of a curse by Poseidon. King Minos of Crete imprisoned this creature in a vast and intricate labyrinth designed by the architect Daedalus. Every few years, Athenian youths were sent into the maze as a form of tribute, and they were invariably lost, wandering the maze until they encountered and were killed by the Minotaur. The hero Theseus eventually ventured into the maze with the aid of Ariadne's thread and managed to slay the Minotaur and escape.

2. Symbolism of the Labyrinth: The maze or labyrinth in which the Minotaur resided has become a symbol of a convoluted or intricate challenge. Over time, the very word "labyrinth" has come to denote any complex system or structure, and the story of the Minotaur adds an element of danger or high stakes to this complexity.

Example Sentence

"Trying to understand the company's bureaucracy felt like navigating a Minotaur's Maze, with one confusing turn leading to another."

The concept of the "Minotaur's Maze" taps into the rich tapestry of Greek mythology to convey the idea of a daunting and perplexing challenge. Just as the ancient labyrinth was a place of danger and confusion, a "Minotaur's Maze" in modern parlance speaks to situations that are fraught with complications, where the path to resolution or clarity seems elusive.

Fairy Godmother

The term "Fairy Godmother" typically refers to someone who helps or rescues another person, often in a generous or timely manner, similar to the magical character in fairy tales who assists those in need with her magical powers. When someone is described as being like a "Fairy Godmother," it means they have provided help, usually unexpectedly or in a way that dramatically changes the situation for the better.

Origin

1. Folk and Fairy Tales: The concept of a Fairy Godmother has its roots in European folk and fairy tales. The most famous portrayal is perhaps in the story of "Cinderella." In this tale, Cinderella's Fairy Godmother magically transforms her tattered clothing into a beautiful ball gown and provides a carriage so she can attend the royal ball, setting the stage for Cinderella to meet the prince.

2. Role and Characteristics: The Fairy Godmother is usually depicted as a kind and benevolent figure. Unlike other magical beings who might have ambiguous or even malevolent intentions, the Fairy Godmother's role is clearly to assist and bestow blessings. This archetype has appeared in various forms across different cultures and tales, always as a guiding or aiding figure.

Example Sentence

"When I was struggling to pay for my tuition, Mrs. Thompson stepped in like a Fairy Godmother and covered the costs."

The idiom "Fairy Godmother" encapsulates the idea of unexpected and benevolent assistance. In a world where challenges can sometimes seem insurmountable, the concept of a Fairy Godmother serves as a reminder of the unexpected kindness and generosity that individuals can extend to one another. It's a symbol of hope, serendipity, and the transformative power of kindness. Whether it's a mentor guiding a protégé, a stranger helping in a time of need, or a friend offering support during challenging times, the "Fairy Godmother" represents the best of human generosity and compassion.

Wear the Cloak of Invisibility

Meaning

The idiom "wear the cloak of invisibility" refers to someone who goes unnoticed or remains hidden, either intentionally or unintentionally. When someone is said to be "wearing the cloak of invisibility," it suggests that they are blending in, avoiding attention, or moving about without being detected.

Origin

1. Mythological and Literary Roots: The concept of invisibility has deep roots in various mythologies and literary traditions. In many tales, characters use cloaks, rings, or other magical objects to become invisible and achieve their goals without detection.

2. Harry Potter Series: The phrase became even more popularized in modern culture due to J.K. Rowling's "Harry Potter" series. In these books, the protagonist possesses a "cloak of invisibility" that allows him to move unseen. Given the widespread influence of the Harry Potter series globally, many people associate the idiom with this literary reference, even though the concept predates Rowling's works.

3. Symbolism of Invisibility: Beyond literal invisibility, the idea also carries a deeper symbolism in society. Many people feel "invisible" due to being marginalized, overlooked, or undervalued. This idiom can resonate with those feelings, expressing a sense of not being seen or recognized.

Example Sentence

"Even though she had great ideas, Jenny often felt like she was wearing the cloak of invisibility during team meetings."

The idiom "wear the cloak of invisibility" encapsulates a range of human experiences, from the desire to move undetected for a specific purpose to the deeper emotional feeling of being overlooked or undervalued. It speaks to the universal desire to be seen, recognized, and valued. While it can sometimes be advantageous to move unnoticed, the phrase also serves as a reminder of the importance of acknowledging and valuing each individual's contributions and presence.

Thank You for Your Support!

I am incredibly grateful that you've chosen "IDIOMS Origins & Meanings" for your linguistic journey. We hope that each page has offered you insights and added a sprinkle of fun to your everyday conversations.

If you've enjoyed this journey as much as I loved creating it, I would be thrilled if you could take a moment to share your experience. Your feedback not only inspires me but also helps fellow language enthusiasts find their way to this unique adventure. Please leave a review using the QR code below or via the following link:

https://mybook.to/IDIOMS-OriginsMeanings

Again, thank you for your support. Keep exploring the fascinating world of idioms!

Check out my next instalment - IDIOMS Origins & Meanings: Volume II

Take a look!